Lotsa Pasta

Michele Anna Jordan

SHADY OAK PRESS

Lotsa Pasta

OVER 100 ELEGANT AND EVERYDAY RECIPES

by Michele Anna Jordan

On Front Cover: Rigatoni with Braised Fennel, Lemon and Fresh Ricotta, page 96
On Page 1: Trenne with Broccoli Raab, Garlic and Soppressatta, page 113

1 2 3 4 5 6 / 12 11 10 09 08
© 2008, 2000 North American Membership Group, Inc.
ISBN: 978-1-58159-367-9
Printed in China
Distributed by:
Sterling Publishing Co., Inc.
387 Park Avenue South
New York, NY 10016-8810

For information about custom editions, special sales, premium and corporate purchases, please contact Sterling Special Sales Department at 800-805-5489 or specialsales@sterlingpublishing.com.

SHADY OAK PRESS

12301 Whitewater Drive
Minnetonka, MN 55343

About the Author

Michele Anna Jordan is the author of many widely-praised books about food, including *The New Cook's Tour of Sonoma*, *Salt & Pepper*, and *California Home Cooking*. She is a columnist for the *Santa Rosa Press Democrat*, North Bay restaurant critic for the *San Francisco Chronicle*, and Culinary Ambassador for Clos du Bois Winery in Sonoma County, California, where she lives.

Tom Carpenter
Creative Director

Jen Weaverling
Managing Editor

Wendy Holdman
Book Design and Production

Linda Steinhoff
Cover Design

Tad Ware & Company, Inc.
Photography, Food Styling, Recipe Testing

$\mathcal{T}$ABLE OF CONTENTS

$\mathcal{I}$NTRODUCTION

Everything you see I owe to spaghetti. — Sophia Loren

In 1950's America, nice girls didn't eat pasta; they didn't even say the word. Pasta was called macaroni and it would make you fat, they were warned. Exceptions were everywhere, of course, especially in communities of Italian

immigrants, but the "official" word of mainstream America was that pasta was something to be indulged in occasionally, if ever. Then, spaghetti was drowned in ground beef and tomato sauce, and elbow macaroni was masked by a golden lake of cheese-flavored cream sauce. Unless you were smart enough to have come from Italian stock, that might have been all you knew of pasta.

Then everything changed. Olive oil came out of the medicine cabinet, garlic out of the dehydrator, tuna out of the can. Farmers' markets began springing up in parking lots, parks and fields. America discovered goat cheese and

mesclun, balsamic vinegar and crème fraîche; we washed it all down with Zinfandel from Sonoma County, Chardonnay and Cabernet Sauvignon from Napa. Life has never been the same.

As you might expect, attitudes toward pasta began to change too. It slowly wound its way to the center of the plate, often several nights a week. It was easy to prepare good pasta at home,

and when the Mediterranean diet was heralded as a healthy alternative to the typical American diet, pasta was considered health food. We should eat mostly carbohydrates, we were told, and use meats and cheeses as condiments, as flavoring for those virtuous noodles and grains. Soon the space pasta took up on market shelves began to expand and there were better choices. Stores specializing in fresh pasta seemed to spring up on every corner. The trendiest among us boasted that we *never* used dried pasta, only fresh, and only what we made ourselves.

Things have settled down since then, and many a pasta machine gathers dust in the back of the pantry or an out-of-the-way cupboard. In the wake of the frenzy, though, pasta has taken a reasonable and essential place in our daily diets, and what is available in the marketplace has never been better.

So we bring you *Lotsa Pasta*. You'll see how to make pasta, you'll see how to select dried pasta (both have their places). And then you'll find dozens and dozens of recipes — some traditional classics you might not know about but *must* have in your repertoire (if nothing else, for the taste alone!), along with exciting new ideas that will become classics in your kitchen.

Pasta is for life. Enjoy both!

—*Michele Anna Jordan*

$\mathcal{P}$ASTA ESSENTIALS

These basic recipes are the building blocks of many recipes, including several pasta recipes in this book. The most important are the rich broths and stocks made from scratch. Sauces in this chapter are simple but versatile: Classic mother recipes that professional chefs use regularly. Your cooking repertoire will expand deliciously as you become comfortable with these essential preparations.

Fresh Egg Pasta, page 11

# PASTA PRIMER

FRESH PASTA

Fresh pasta, tender and rich with golden egg yolks, is at its best a delicate pleasure. Unless you have a store near you that makes fresh pasta daily, it should be made at home. You can find it in most supermarkets, packaged in plastic containers; but most brands are dismal, with thick noodles that turn gummy when cooked. They miss the point entirely.

Many professional chefs and food writers believe that fresh pasta should be made with only all-purpose white flour and eggs, but I've found that adding from one-quarter to one-third semolina flour produces a wonderfully tender pasta with a bit more structure than that made only with all-purpose flour. The recipes in this book use this formula.

There are many pasta machines available to the home cook, but I've never found one I like better than the hand-cranked Atlas, one of the first to appear in the marketplace. It is inexpensive, easy to use and reliable. For the best results, I recommend this machine and the best ingredients you can get: eggs from the farmers' market, good flour that hasn't been sitting on the shelf too long, and Diamond Crystal brand kosher salt, which dissolves more quickly than table salt, most sea salts and other kosher salts.

DRIED PASTA

Commercial dried pasta is made with winter wheat (hard durum wheat) and water. All pastas are not created equal; there is no single process that all producers follow. Some pastas are flash-dried in mere seconds, others allowed to dry for several days. Those that are dried more slowly generally have more flavor and may have higher nutritional values as well, because their nutrients are not destroyed by the rapid drying process.

In general, pastas imported from Italy are far superior to those made in the United States. There is a single exception: Coppola brand pasta introduced recently by the famous director's food enterprise.

What makes a good dried pasta? Producers must begin with high-quality wheat that has been milled recently rather than weeks or even months before it is used. Water should not have unpleasant flavors. The best artisan pastas, such as those produced by Rustichella d'Abruzzo, are extruded through dies made of bronze, which contribute a rough texture to the surface of the pasta. We've all had noodles that are slick, smooth, and shiny; sauces don't adhere to them. Sauces embrace pastas with a roughened texture; flavors and ingredients are evenly distributed throughout the dish.

The pastas from Rustichella d'Abruzzo are slowly dried for as long as 56 hours, a gentle process that creates a satisfying product. Not only is it higher in nutrients than flash-dried pastas, its fuller taste is so satisfying that you will be less inclined to eat more than is wise, a tendency with pastas that aren't as good as they should be because you keep anticipating a satisfaction, a satiation, that never comes.

Rustichella d'Abruzzo, once hard to find, is now available in most states, and all 42 shapes that are imported to the United States are available through the Internet at www.tavola.com or www.chefshop.com.

And yes, premium Italian pastas are more expensive than most domestic brands. (Coppola's is priced about the same as a good import.) If you wonder if it's worth it, do a taste test. Buy similar shapes — a good imported brand and a common domestic brand — cook them in the same amount of water and salt, and taste them, unsauced, side by side.

DeCecco, Felicetti, Delverde and Barilla make good, moderately priced pastas.

WHAT ABOUT FLAVORED PASTAS?

As fresh pasta became enormously popular, so did a rainbow of colors and flavors. Cookbooks include recipes for pasta flavored with tomato paste, dried tomatoes, herbs, spices, spinach, sage, carrots, beets, saffron, pumpkin, olives and squid ink. (In the spirit of full disclosure, I should tell you that I have written two such books.) So what about it? Is it a good idea?

In the end, I can't say that I think the flavor contributed warrants much trouble. Ruby-red pasta, colored by puréed roasted beets, is certainly a thrill to the eye, and I love to serve hauntingly black squid-ink pasta on Halloween. But some ingredients, including basil and garlic (two of the most common seasonings in pasta), often contribute a mildly unpleasant element. In general, my advice is to make simple fresh pasta, golden from good egg yolks, and add flavor with a good sauce.

To make good pasta at home, follow a few simple rules (my from-scratch recipe follows), practice, and don't worry if you have to discard your first batch or two. There's a learning curve, but it's actually pretty short.

$\mathcal{M}$AKING PASTA FROM SCRATCH

The taste of fresh, made-from-scratch pasta really has no match. Making fresh pasta isn't really all that difficult, either, if you follow a few simple guidelines (below) and have a good basic recipe (also included). Here are the guidelines:

- Have everything you need at hand before you begin: not just the ingredients, but also a cutting board, clean kitchen towels for covering the pasta, a rack of some sort for drying, and plenty of extra flour for dusting work surfaces.
- After kneading the pasta dough, let it rest, covered, 30 to 60 minutes; the gluten will relax and it will be easier to work the dough.
- Allow pasta sheets to dry for several minutes before cutting them. Allow cut pasta to dry for about 30 minutes before cooking it.
- Cook fresh pasta in plenty of rapidly boiling salted water until it is tender. *Al dente* — literally, "to the tooth" — applies only to dried pasta.
- Drain — but do not rinse — the pasta.

FRESH EGG PASTA

There is, of course, no substitute for fresh pasta. It's not difficult to make, though it takes a little practice to learn how the dough changes as you work with it. This recipe is designed for use with an Atlas hand-cranked pasta machine, but should work for you on other brand machines too. Because this recipe includes a significant percentage of semolina flour, and is therefore a fairly stiff dough, it would be difficult to make this pasta by hand.

ONE-EGG PASTA

$1/3$ cup semolina flour
$2/3$ cup unbleached all-purpose flour
$1/4$ teaspoon kosher (coarse) salt
   1   egg, room temperature
   2   teaspoons water

2 main course servings.

Per serving: 270 calories, 3 g total fat (1 g saturated fat), 105 mg cholesterol, 230 mg sodium, 2 g fiber.

TWO-EGG PASTA

2/3 cup semolina flour

1 1/2 cups unbleached all-purpose flour

3/4 teaspoon kosher (coarse) salt

2 eggs, room temperature

1 tablespoon water

4 main course servings.

Per serving: 290 calories, 3 g total fat (1 g saturated fat), 105 mg cholesterol, 325 mg sodium, 2 g fiber.

THREE-EGG PASTA

1 cup semolina flour

2 cups unbleached all-purpose flour

1 teaspoon kosher (coarse) salt

3 eggs, room temperature

2 tablespoons water

6 main course servings.

Per serving: 270 calories, 3 g total fat (1 g saturated fat), 105 mg cholesterol, 290 mg sodium, 2 g fiber.

INSTRUCTIONS FOR MAKING PASTA

❶ Combine flours and salt in food processor; pulse 3 or 4 times. With machine running, add egg(s) and water. Continue processing about 45 seconds or until dough forms soft ball, stopping to scrape bowl with rubber spatula if necessary.

❷ Sprinkle flour on clean work surface. Knead dough 2 or 3 times. Break dough into 3 equal pieces. Pat dough into rectangle; flatten dough with palm to 3/8-inch thickness.

❸ Set pasta machine on widest setting; crank dough through machine 10 to 12 times, dusting with flour and folding in half after each pass (dough will become a lighter color and will begin to feel smooth and elastic).

❹ Set dough on floured work surface; cover with clean kitchen towel. Repeat until all dough has been kneaded. Let dough rest 1 hour.

❺ Pass dough through each pasta machine setting, working from widest to narrowest, 3 or 4 times, folding dough in half or in thirds each time so a long ribbon (about 4 inches wide) is formed. Cut dough into desired noodle shape.

Preparation time: 30 minutes. Ready to serve: 1 hour, 40 minutes.

TIPS FOR COOKING DRIED PASTA

Often there just isn't time to make pasta from scratch. And that's no sin, with so many good dried pastas on the market today. But you have to know how to cook it. Here are some guidelines:

- For one pound of dried pasta, use a large pot that will hold 5 to 6 quarts of water, and be sure the water has come to a rolling boil before adding the pasta. Pasta cooked in too little water becomes mushy.

- Salt the water using at least 1 tablespoon kosher salt; 2 tablespoons is better. Salt allows the flavor of the wheat to blossom. Pasta cooked in unsalted water is bland and flat, and no amount of salt added later, and no sauce, can coax out the missing flavor.

- Stir the pasta with a long-handled pasta fork or wooden spoon to move it around in the pot; this also separates individual pieces or strands so that they don't stick together.

- It's helpful to cover the pot after adding pasta until the water returns to a boil.

- Stir pasta two or three times as it cooks.

- Taste, taste, taste! *Al dente* is a subjective evaluation: It means the pasta should be tender with a bit of pleasant resistance at its very center. The only way to achieve this is to taste the pasta several times during the final minute or two of cooking.

- To drain a pasta that you will serve immediately, set a colander over a wide shallow bowl set in the sink, being certain the drain is not covered. Pour the pasta into the colander so the pasta water heats the bowl beneath. Shake excess water off the pasta, move it aside, and using protection against the hot bowl, pour out the water. Set the bowl on a work surface, put the pasta in it and add the sauce.

- To serve a pasta at room temperature or as an ingredient in another recipe, such as a soufflé or frittata, rinse the pasta in cool water, tossing the pasta as you do. The purpose here is to cool the pasta off and prevent it from sticking.

Turn it into a bowl, and toss it with a very small amount of olive oil to avoid it sticking together.

- If a sauce, such as pesto, seems a little thick or stiff, stir in 2 or 3 tablespoons of the cooking water.

- Don't use too much sauce.

- Add sauce and serve your pasta immediately after it is cooked. If necessary, keep cooked pasta hot by draping a cloth napkin or clean kitchen towel over the bowl.

- Pay attention to seasonal ingredients. Not only do foods taste best in their own true season — asparagus and peas in the spring, basil in the summer, pumpkin and cauliflower in the fall and winter — they taste best when paired with their seasonal companions. Use tomatoes in the summer and save dried tomatoes with their intense concentrated flavors for the cooler months, paired with other winter foods such as cauliflower and mushrooms.

Matching Shape and Sauce

Historically, pasta shapes were created for specific purposes: fresh flat sheets for cutting and folding into tortellini, ravioli and other filled pastas; seed shapes for soup; flat noodles whose broad surfaces hold a creamy sauce; curly strands, both short and long, whose twists and turns trap morsels of meat and vegetables so that the sauce is evenly distributed; and thin noodles to which tomato sauce and olive oil easily cling.

The Italian names for specific pasta shapes are frequently whimsical — little ears, angel's hair, priest stranglers, little butterflies — but the shapes themselves always serve a purpose on the palate as well as the plate. You will be most pleased with your results if you combine pastas and sauces based on these traditional pairings.

- Pair fresh pastas, which are porous, with cream sauces, butter sauces and meat sauces. Do not pair fresh pastas with oil-based sauces.
- Use Capelli d'Angelo, the popular angel hair pasta, in soups and, perhaps, frittatas and soufflés. Sauces are too heavy for this pasta.
- Spaghettini is thinner than spaghetti and is excellent with light sauces such as pesto.
- Spaghetti is a good all-purpose noodle.
- Fusilli lunghi, also called fusilli col buco, is a long, coiled strand; it is perfectly suited to chunky sauces, such as ragu.
- Serve fettuccine with light cream-based sauces, such as Alfredo.
- Tagliatelle is twice as wide as fettuccine; its classic pairing is with Bolognese sauce.
- Papardelle is the widest noodle, and it can be paired with substantial sauces such as ragu, as well as butter-based sauces.
- Use seed-shaped pastas in soups, soufflés and frittatas, or sauce them very simply with butter and serve as a side dish.
- Pair tube-shaped pastas with ingredients of similar size; tube pastas work well with many olive oil-based sauces.
- Short strands, such as gemelli, al ceppo, casareccia, and those charming priest chokers known as strozzapreti, are best paired with ingredients of similar length and width, such as julienned vegetables.
- Do not use instant lasagne noodles. They lack appealing texture.

ESSENTIAL SAUCES AND STOCKS

Now that you know the essentials of both fresh and dried pasta, how to cook them and what you might pair them with, here are sauce and stock recipes every pasta lover needs in his or her repertoire.

BECHAMEL SAUCE

This classic sauce is both simple and essential; it takes just a few minutes to make. Bechamel sauce adds richness to traditional lasagna, but in a pinch it can be used for a quick pasta by adding grated cheese and fresh or frozen peas.

 3 tablespoons butter
 1 shallot, minced
 2 tablespoons all-purpose flour
 1/2 teaspoon kosher (coarse) salt
    Freshly ground pepper to taste
 1 cup whipping cream

❶ In small saucepan, melt butter over medium-high heat; add shallot. Sauté about 5 minutes or until softened. Sprinkle flour over shallot and butter; simmer 2 minutes. Add 1/2 teaspoon salt; season with pepper. Whisk in cream.

❷ Reduce heat to low; simmer about 2 minutes or until thickened slightly. Remove from heat.

1 1/8 cups.
Preparation time: 5 minutes. Ready to serve: 15 minutes.
Per cup: 275 calories, 25 g total fat (17 g saturated fat), 90 mg cholesterol, 270 mg sodium, 0 g fiber.

CLARIFIED BUTTER

When you heat butter until it is melted, milk solids sink to the bottom and impurities rise to the surface, where they are easy to skim off. By removing these elements, you have pure butter fat, which can be heated to higher temperatures than butter that has not been clarified. Butter with milk solids will burn.

1   cup butter

❶ In medium saucepan, melt butter over medium heat. Skim and discard foam from top of melted butter. Carefully pour melted butter into small container, being careful to leave milk solids in bottom of pan. (It might be necessary to spoon off final bit of melted butter rather than pour it.) Clarified butter will keep, covered and refrigerated, up to 2 weeks.

3/4 cup.
Preparation time: 15 minutes. Ready to serve: 15 minutes.
Per teaspoon: 40 calories, 5 g total fat (2.5 g saturated fat), 10 mg cholesterol, 0 mg sodium, 0 g fiber.

TOMATO CONCASSE

This light, uncooked tomato sauce, best when made with homegrown ripe tomatoes, is often used as the foundation of a more complex recipe but it can also be tossed with hot pasta for a simple summer dish.

1   lb. ripe tomatoes
    Kosher (coarse) salt to taste

❶ To peel tomato, press onto tines of dinner fork; hold tomato close to burner on stove. Turn slowly, searing skin all around. Do not let tomato blacken. Set aside until tomato is cool enough to handle. Remove skin.

❷ With paring knife, cut out core of each tomato; cut tomato in half through its equator. Hold tomato half in hand with rounded side against your palm; gently squeeze and discard seeds and juice.

❸ With sharp knife, chop tomatoes until nearly reduced to purée. Scoop pulp (also known as *concassé*) into bowl; season with salt.

1 cup.
Preparation time: 20 minutes. Ready to serve: 20 minutes.
Per cup: 30 calories, 0.5 g total fat (1 g saturated fat), 0 mg cholesterol, 300 mg sodium, 2 g fiber.

PRESERVED LEMONS

When lemons are marinated in a substantial quantity of salt and lemon juice, their thick skins soften and their sour taste mellows. A traditional condiment in Moroccan cuisine, preserved lemons have become increasingly popular in the United States and with good reason: They add a bright, zesty intensity that many people find irresistible…and perfect to pair with pasta recipes.

3   lemons
    Boiling water
3   tablespoons kosher (coarse) salt
2   teaspoons sugar
1/2 cup fresh lemon juice

❶ In deep bowl, soak lemons in boiling water 15 minutes. Drain water; repeat. Drain again; dry lemons. With sharp knife, cut each lemon into 6 lengthwise slices. Carefully remove seeds.

❷ In small bowl, combine lemon slices, salt and sugar; toss gently and quickly. Pack lemons into 2 (1/2 pint) glass jars. Pour lemon juice over lemons; cover jar openings with plastic wrap. Close jars tightly with lids.

❸ Set jars in cool, dark cupboard at least 5 days. Twice each day, in morning and evening, shake jars to help lemons age evenly. After 5 days, lemons should be completely tender and ready for use. Keep in refrigerator 6 to 8 weeks.

2 (1/2 pint) jars.

Preparation time: 45 minutes. Ready to serve: 5 days.

Per 1 cup serving: 4 calories, 0 g total fat (0 g saturated fat), 0 mg cholesterol, 435 mg sodium, 0 g fiber.

CHICKEN STOCK

When it comes to home cooking, chicken stock is the best all-purpose stock (professional chefs rely on veal stock). Chicken stock is easy and inexpensive to prepare, and chicken is available virtually everywhere. Keep in mind, though, that your stock cannot be more flavorful than the ingredients that make it; try to use free-range chickens, which have much more flavor than commercial, "factory-raised" chickens. You will use this stock in a wide range of recipes, including some of the pastas in this book.

- 2 tablespoons olive oil
- 4 lbs. chicken backs and necks
  Kosher (coarse) salt to taste
  Freshly ground pepper to taste
- 1 yellow onion, quartered
- 1 carrot, cut into chunks
- 1 rib celery, cut into chunks
- 1 bouquet garni

❶ In large pot, heat oil over medium-high heat until hot; add chicken and brown evenly. Season with salt and pepper; add onion, carrot, celery and garni, sauté 15 minutes. Add 3 quarts water.

❷ Increase heat to high; bring to a boil. Reduce heat to medium and simmer, partially covered, 2 1/2 hours. Remove from heat; let cool slightly. Strain through fine sieve; discard solids and pour liquid back into stockpot.

❸ Reheat liquid over high heat until boiling; reduce heat to simmer. Simmer until stock is reduced by one-third, about 20 minutes. Remove from heat; cool to room temperature. Store in refrigerator up to 5 days.

❹ Before using stock, lift off and discard hard layer of fat that will form on top as stock chills. Chicken stock can be frozen up to 3 months.

6 to 7 cups.

Preparation time: 10 minutes. Ready to serve: 3 hours.

Per serving: 35 calories, 2 g total fat (.5 g saturated fat), 0 mg cholesterol, 830 mg sodium, 0 g fiber.

BEEF STOCK

Beef stock contributes a depth of flavor and a structure to recipes that is otherwise impossible to achieve. Beef stock is not difficult to make, and actual hands-on work is minimal. Always make more than you'll need for a single recipe so that you'll have plenty left over to freeze. Once again — this is a stock you will use in a wide range of recipes, including some of the pastas in this book.

2   tablespoons olive oil
5   lbs. beef shanks or chuck, cut into chunks
     Kosher (coarse) salt to taste
     Freshly ground pepper to taste
3   lbs. veal bones or beef marrow bones
2   yellow onions, quartered
1   carrot, cut into chunks
1   rib celery, cut into chunks
3   plum tomatoes, halved
1   bouquet garni

❶ In large pot, heat oil over medium-high heat; add beef and brown evenly. Season with salt and pepper; add bones. Cook 5 minutes. Add onion, carrot, celery, tomatoes and garni. Cook about 15 minutes or until vegetables soften. Add 1 gallon water.

❷ Increase heat to high; bring to a boil. Reduce heat to medium and simmer, partially covered, 2$1/2$ hours. Strain stock through fine sieve; discard solids and return liquid to pot.

❸ Reheat stock over high heat until boiling; reduce to simmer. Simmer about 20 minutes or until stock is reduced by one-third. Remove from heat; cool to room temperature. Store in refrigerator up to 5 days.

❹ Before using stock, lift off and discard hard layer of fat that will form on top as stock chills. Stock can be frozen up to 3 months.

6 to 7 cups.
Preparation time: 10 minutes. Ready to serve: 3 hours.
Per serving: 35 calories, 2 g total fat (1 g saturated fat), 0 mg cholesterol, 830 mg sodium, 0 g fiber.

Soups

Soup with pasta can be an elegant
first course, a bone-warming main
course, or a restorative snack when
you're recuperating from anything
that ails you. Traditionally, seed
pastas and the smaller shapes are
made for soup, and there are dozens
of versions in Italy. But you can
always use thin strands such as
angel hair or spaghettini, and some
recipes call for wider noodles.

Winter Squash Broth with Tortellini and Greens, page 36

RISO AND PEA SOUP

Risi e bisi is a classic dish of Venice, served in the spring to honor St. Mark. This version uses pasta instead of rice, and the main reason to make it is because there's a harvest of fresh spring peas in the garden but no rice in the pantry. This version is not as creamy as the one made with rice because pasta does not break down in the same way as the grain. But it's a very good soup, best made with young peas.

6	oz. riso (seed-shaped pasta)
1	tablespoon kosher (coarse) salt plus more to taste
4	tablespoons unsalted butter
1	shallot, minced
1½	cups freshly shelled peas
3	cups *Chicken Stock* (page 22)
10	fresh mint leaves
1	tablespoon minced fresh Italian parsley
1	tablespoon minced fresh chives
½	cup grated Pecorino cheese (2 oz.)
	Freshly ground pepper to taste

❶ Fill large pot two-thirds full of water; add 1 tablespoon salt. Bring to a boil over high heat. Cook riso according to package directions; drain. Set aside.

❷ Meanwhile, melt 2 tablespoons of the butter in medium skillet over medium-low heat. Add shallot; cook about 4 minutes or until soft and fragrant. Add peas and sauté an additional 4 minutes, stirring constantly. Add Chicken Stock; increase heat to medium-high. Bring stock to a boil; reduce heat to medium-low. Simmer about 4 minutes or until peas are almost tender. Stir cooked pasta into stock; simmer an additional 5 minutes.

❸ Stack mint leaves on work surface. Using very sharp knife, cut into very thin crosswise strips. Stir mint, parsley and chives into stock; season with salt and pepper. Remove from heat; stir cheese into soup. Ladle into warm bowls. Divide remaining 2 tablespoons butter among servings and use tip of spoon to swirl — not mix — butter into soup.

4 to 6 servings.

Preparation time: 20 minutes. Ready to serve: 40 minutes.

Per serving: 395 calories, 17 g total fat (10 g saturated fat), 40 mg cholesterol, 1230 mg sodium, 5 g fiber.

PASTA AND BEAN SOUP

The best gift you can give a soup is good stock, and it is particularly true with a soup such as this one. Made with water or a weak broth, the soup is nowhere near as rich and satisfying as when it is made with good homemade beef stock, the recipe for which you will find on page 23.

1¹/2 cups (about 10 oz.) dried cranberry beans or cannellini beans
  3 tablespoons olive oil
 ¹/4 cup yellow onion, minced
  1 carrot, minced
  1 rib celery, minced
 ¹/4 lb. pancetta, minced
  1 cup *Tomato Concassé* (page 19)
  1 tablespoon kosher (coarse) salt plus more to taste
     Freshly ground pepper to taste
  4 cups *Beef Stock* (page 23) or 1 (14-oz.) can beef broth plus
       4 cups water
  4 Italian parsley sprigs
  8 oz. canneroni (short tube-shaped pasta)
  2 tablespoons minced fresh Italian parsley
  2 tablespoons extra-virgin olive oil
  1 block Parmigiano-Reggiano cheese (3 oz.)

❶ Soak beans overnight in large pot with water 2 inches above beans. Drain beans and cover with fresh water; cook over medium-high heat about 1 hour or until very plump and tender. Drain.

❷ Heat 3 tablespoons olive oil in large pot over medium-low heat until hot; add onion, carrot and celery. Sauté 12 to 15 minutes or until vegetables are soft and tender, stirring occasionally; add pancetta. Sauté an additional 5 minutes or until pancetta is completely translucent; drain fat. Stir in Tomato Concassé; season with salt and pepper to taste. Add Beef Stock, cooked beans and parsley sprigs; bring to a boil. Reduce heat to medium-low; simmer 20 minutes.

③ Fill large pot two-thirds full of water; add 1 tablespoon salt. Bring to a boil over high heat. Cook canneroni according to package directions; drain. Rinse thoroughly in cool water and drain pasta.

④ Remove and discard parsley sprigs from stock. Using an immersion blender inserted directly into pot, purée about one-fourth of the soup. Stir soup to blend stock with purée. Stir in minced parsley and pasta; let stand, covered, 5 to 10 minutes. Ladle into warm soup bowls; drizzle 1 to 2 teaspoons extra-virgin olive oil over each bowl. Grate cheese over each portion.

4 to 6 servings.

Preparation time: 20 minutes. Ready to serve: 45 minutes.

Per serving: 700 calories, 21 g total fat (4 g saturated fat), 10 mg cholesterol, 1200 mg sodium, 16 g fiber.

ACINI DI PEPE WITH LEMON BROTH AND BLACK PEPPER

In this refreshing and satisfying soup, you can use any of the seed pastas, but the round nuggets of acini di pepe are the ones I prefer. Because of their shape, they add a bit more volume than the flatter seeds.

2 sprigs Italian parsley

2 sprigs thyme

2 sprigs oregano

2 sprigs basil

1 tablespoon kosher (coarse) salt plus more to taste

6 oz. acini di pepe (peppercorn-shaped pasta)

4 cups *Chicken Stock* (page 22)

2 garlic cloves, crushed

2 tablespoons grated lemon peel

2 tablespoons fresh lemon juice

Freshly ground pepper to taste

2 tablespoons fresh-snipped chives

1 block Parmigiano-Reggiano or dry Monterey Jack cheese (3 oz.)

❶ Tie herb sprigs together in bundle.

❷ Fill large pot two-thirds full of water; add 1 tablespoon salt. Bring to a boil over high heat. Cook acini de pepe according to package directions; drain. Set aside.

❸ In medium saucepan, heat herbs, Chicken Stock, garlic and lemon peel over medium heat to boiling. Cover and remove from heat; let steep 15 minutes. Return to medium heat; remove and discard herb sprigs. Stir in lemon juice and pasta; season with salt and pepper. Ladle into warm soup bowls; sprinkle with chives. Grate cheese over each portion.

4 servings.

Preparation time: 5 minutes. Ready to serve: 25 minutes.

Per serving: 310 calories, 9 g total fat (5 g saturated fat), 15 mg cholesterol, 1605 mg sodium, 1.5 g fiber.

CLAMS AND PASTA IN TOMATO BROTH

For a more elegant soup: Remove all the clams, except one per serving, from their shells. After ladling the soup into individual soup plates, set a single clam on top as garnish. For a more rustic soup, leave all the clams in their shells and be sure to provide a big bowl for discarding shells.

- 5 lbs. small hard-shell Manila clams in the shell, thoroughly scrubbed
- 2 cups dry white wine
- 2 shallots
- 2 tablespoons olive oil
- 8 garlic cloves, minced
- 2 *Preserved Lemon* wedges (page 20), minced
- 1/2 teaspoon crushed red pepper
  Freshly ground pepper to taste
- 2 cups *Tomato Concassé* (page 19)
- 1 tablespoon kosher (coarse) salt
- 6 oz. farfalline or other small pasta
- 3 tablespoons minced fresh Italian parsley
- 4 to 6 *Preserved Lemon* wedges

❶ Place clams in large pot; add wine. Bring to a boil over high heat. Cover and cook 4 to 5 minutes or until all clam shells are open. Remove from heat; using slotted spoon, transfer clams to large bowl.

❷ Strain cooking liquid into bowl; set aside. Rinse out pot. Sauté shallots in olive oil over medium heat about 7 minutes or until soft. Add garlic; sauté 2 minutes. Add minced Preserved Lemon wedges and crushed red pepper; season with pepper. Pour in reserved cooking liquid; simmer 5 minutes or until liquid is reduced by one-third. Stir in Tomato Concassé. Simmer 5 minutes.

❸ Meanwhile, fill another large pot two-thirds full of water; add 1 tablespoon salt. Bring to a boil over high heat. Cook farfelline according

to package directions; drain. Set aside. Set one-third of the clams in their shells in medium saucepan, discarding any that have not opened. Remove clams from remaining two-thirds clam shells; stir into tomato mixture. Add parsley and cooked pasta; stir over medium heat until heated through. Cover and cook clams in their shells over medium heat until heated through. Ladle tomato mixture into large soup bowls. Divide clams in their shells among bowls. Garnish each portion with Preserved Lemon wedge.

4 to 6 servings.

Preparation time: 30 minutes. Ready to serve: 1 hour.

Per serving: 355 calories, 9 g total fat (1 g saturated fat), 30 mg cholesterol, 860 mg sodium, 3.5 g fiber.

ZUCCHINI, SAUSAGE AND ORECCHIETTE IN SPICY BEEF BROTH

These vegetables, sausage and pasta are similarly shaped — round like coins — creating a visual pattern in the bowl and on the palate that I find quite pleasing. You can, of course, use another pasta, though the orecchiette are so ideally suited that I don't recommend substituting.

10 cups *Beef Stock* (page 23)
 1 small tarragon sprig
 1 small chervil sprig
 1 teaspoon crushed red pepper
 1 tablespoon kosher (coarse) salt
 6 oz. orecchiette (disk-shaped pasta)
 4 (1-lb.) spicy Italian sausages
 2 bunches green onions, white and palest green parts only,
      thinly sliced
 1 tablespoon *Clarified Butter* (page 18)
 4 (5-inch) zucchini, cut into 1/2-inch rounds
    Freshly ground pepper to taste
 1 block freshly grated Parmigiano-Reggiano cheese (3 oz.)

❶ In large pot, heat Beef Stock, tarragon, chervil and crushed red pepper to a boil over high heat. Reduce heat to low; simmer 15 minutes. Remove and discard herb sprigs; set stock aside.

❷ Fill another large pot two-thirds full of water; add 1 tablespoon salt. Bring to a boil over high heat. Cook orecchiette according to package directions; drain. Do not rinse.

❸ Meanwhile, use fork to prick sausages in several places; fry in medium skillet over medium heat until browned and most of the fat has been released. Transfer sausages to paper towels; cool. Drain off all but 2 tablespoons fat. Return pan to medium-low heat; add onions. Sauté about 15 minutes or until soft and fragrant. Stir mixture into stock. Cut sausage into 1/4-inch rounds; add to stock. Simmer over medium-low heat 15 minutes.

④ Melt Clarified Butter in medium skillet over medium-high heat; add zucchini. Sauté, tossing frequently, 3 to 4 minutes or until zucchini is just barely tender. Season with pepper. Stir zucchini and cooked pasta into stock; simmer 5 minutes. Ladle into soup bowls. Sprinkle grated cheese over each portion, passing remaining cheese and grater.

8 servings.
Preparation time: 20 minutes. Ready to serve: 1 hour.

Per serving: 545 calories, 25 g total fat (10 g saturated fat), 70 mg cholesterol, 3430 mg sodium, 4 g fiber.

WINTER SQUASH BROTH WITH TORTELLINI AND GREENS

If you're pinched for time but really want to make this flavorful winter soup, you can use a good commercial tortellini instead of making it yourself. Agnolotti — half-moons of filled pasta — also look beautiful in the golden broth. Pages 24 and 25 show this wonderful soup in all its glory.

1   (4-lb.) winter squash, such as Tahitian Melon, banana or acorn
4   tablespoons olive oil
1   cup onion, minced
    Kosher (coarse) salt to taste
    Freshly ground pepper to taste
3   garlic cloves
4   cups sliced Swiss chard
    Cheese Tortellini, cooked until tender (recipe follows)

❶ To make broth, cut squash in half; scoop out seeds and fibers. Cut into 1-inch pieces. Use sharp paring knife or vegetable peeler to peel each piece of squash; cut into medium dice.

❷ Pour 2 tablespoons of the olive oil into large pot over medium-low heat. Add onion; sauté 5 minutes or until softened. Reduce heat to low; add squash. Cook 25 minutes, partially covered, until tender. Season with salt and pepper.

❸ Pour 2 quarts water over squash. Increase heat to high; heat to a boil. Reduce heat. Simmer, partially covered, 1½ hours. Strain broth through fine sieve. Clean pot; return broth to pot. Cook over medium heat until reduced by half (6 cups).

❹ Heat remaining 2 tablespoons olive oil in medium skillet over medium-low heat. Add garlic; sauté 30 seconds. Add greens; toss with garlic. Cover pan; cook 4 minutes or until leaves are wilted. Stir cooked greens into squash broth. Add cooked tortellini; heat through. Ladle into warm soup bowls.

8 servings.
Preparation time: 45 minutes. Ready to serve: 2 hours, 45 minutes.

Per serving: 600 calories, 38 g total fat (13 g saturated fat), 155 mg cholesterol, 745 mg sodium, 5 g fiber.

CHEESE TORTELLINI

1	recipe *One-Egg Pasta* (page 11), rolled into 4x12-inch strips
3/4	cup young chèvre (3 oz.)
3/4	cup fresh ricotta, drained (3 oz.)
1/2	cup Pecorino Romano cheese (2 oz.)
1/2	cup imported Gorgonzola (2 oz.)
1	tablespoon minced Italian parsley
1	egg, beaten
	Freshly ground pepper to taste
1	tablespoon kosher (coarse) salt

❶ Set pasta on lightly floured work surface. With 2-inch round cookie cutter, cut 48 circles. Cover circles with clean kitchen towel.

❷ In medium bowl, use fork to combine chèvre, ricotta, Pecorino Romano, and Gorgonzola. Mix in parsley and egg; season with pepper. Set aside.

❸ Fill small bowl with water. Set several pasta circles on work surface; brush each one lightly with water. Use tip of teaspoon to place dollop of filling in center of each circle. Fold circle in half, press edges together; wrap half-circle around tip of your finger, pinching two ends together. Repeat until all circles have been filled. Set tortellini in single layer on work surface and let dry 30 minutes. (Prepare soup while tortellini dry.)

❹ Fill medium pot two-thirds full of water; add 1 tablespoon salt. Bring to a boil over high heat. When water boils, cook tortellini about 3 minutes or until pasta is tender. Using a slotted spoon, transfer tortellini to warm serving bowl. (Keep tortellini hot while preparing soup.)

6 servings.

Prep time: 1 hour, 45 minutes. Ready to serve: 2 hours, 15 minutes.

Per serving: 465 calories, 22 g total fat (14 g saturated fat), 200 mg cholesterol, 1170 mg sodium, 1 g fiber.

SALADS

Light, refreshing, interesting, flavorful … all these words describe the pasta salads here. A pasta salad should almost always be served at room temperature (for maximum flavor), and its dressing should be light and delicate, usually some sort of vinaigrette. Leftover pasta salads should, of course, be covered and stored in the refrigerator; but return them to room temperature before serving again.

Chilled Shellfish Salad, page 50

CAESAR SALAD PASTA

This recipe is one of my old standbys, something I often make for myself after a long day of writing. You will love this special pasta salad too — after a long day of your work. Caesar Salad Pasta is perfect on a hot summer night, refreshing but satisfying.

Parmigiano-Reggiano Croutons (recipe follows)
2   pasteurized eggs
1   tablespoon kosher (coarse) salt
8 to 10   oz. dried spaghettini
1/2   cup extra-virgin olive oil
3   garlic cloves, minced
3   anchovy fillets, minced
1   head romaine lettuce, washed, cut into 1-inch strips
3   tablespoons fresh lemon juice
Freshly ground pepper to taste
3/4   cup freshly grated dry Monterey Jack cheese (3 oz.)

❶ Prepare Parmigiano-Reggiano Croutons. Set aside. In small saucepan, cover eggs with 1 inch water. Heat to boiling; cook 1 minute. Remove from heat; drain. Set aside.

❷ Fill large pot two-thirds full of water; add 1 tablespoon salt. Bring to a boil over high heat. Cook spaghettini according to package directions; drain. Rinse and drain thoroughly in cool water.

❸ Pour olive oil into large bowl; mix in garlic and anchovies. Add romaine and pasta; toss until evenly coated. Add lemon juice; toss again. Break eggs, one at a time, into salad; toss thoroughly. Season with pepper, 3/4 cup cheese and one-half of the croutons; toss again. Divide evenly among serving plates; top each portion with croutons.

3 servings.
Preparation time: 20 minutes. Ready to serve: 35 minutes

Per serving: 1230 calories, 90 g total fat (18.5 g saturated fat), 180 mg cholesterol, 1330 mg sodium, 7 g fiber.

PARMIGIANO-REGGIANO CROUTONS

$^1/_3$ cup extra-virgin olive oil

  2 garlic cloves, minced

  3 cups bread cubes from day-old country-style bread

  1 teaspoon kosher (coarse) salt

  Freshly ground pepper to taste

$^1/_4$ cup grated dry Monterey Jack cheese (1 oz.)

❶ Heat oven to 300°F. In large jar or other lidded container, combine olive oil, garlic and bread cubes; season with 1 teaspoon salt and pepper. Shake container vigorously until bread has absorbed all of the oil and cubes are evenly coated. Add cheese and shake again.

❷ Spread bread cubes on baking sheet and bake about 15 minutes, stirring occasionally, until cubes are dry and slightly golden brown. Let cool to room temperature.

3 servings.

Preparation time: 20 minutes. Ready to serve: 30 minutes.

Per serving: 315 calories, 27 g total fat (5 g saturated fat), 10 mg cholesterol, 720 mg sodium, 1 g fiber.

SUMMER PASTA SALAD

For the best results, use an excellent pasta made in the traditional way, using bronze dies and dried slowly in open air. Cencioni means little rags, which refers to the pasta's uneven, flat shape.

- 3 red bell peppers, seeded, oven-roasted, peeled*
- 4 plum tomatoes, oven-roasted, peeled**
- 6 garlic cloves, thinly sliced
- 3 oz. oil-cured black olives, pitted, sliced in half lengthwise
- 1 1/2 cups fresh mozzarella, drained, sliced (6 oz.)
- 1/3 cup red wine vinegar
  Freshly ground pepper to taste
- 1 tablespoon kosher (coarse) salt plus more to taste
- 1 (8.8-oz.) pkg. cencioni pasta, farfallone, or farfalle
- 1/2 cup plus 3 tablespoons extra-virgin olive oil
- 1 tablespoon minced fresh Italian parsley
- 2 teaspoons fresh oregano leaves

❶ Slice bell peppers into wide strips; place in shallow serving bowl. Break tomatoes into chunks; add to peppers along with garlic, olives and mozzarella. Toss gently; pour vinegar over vegetables. Sprinkle with pepper; set aside.

❷ Fill large pot two-thirds full of water; add 1 tablespoon salt. Bring to a boil over high heat. Cook cencioni according to package directions; drain. Rinse and drain thoroughly in cool water; add to pepper mixture.

❸ Add remaining 1/2 cup olive oil, parsley and oregano; season with salt. If salad is tart, add a little more olive oil.

4 servings.
Preparation Time: 1 hour, 10 minutes. Ready to serve: 2 hours.
Per serving: 600 calories, 34 g total fat (6 g saturated fat), 10 mg cholesterol, 755 mg sodium, 4 g fiber.

TIPS *To roast peppers, heat oven to 375°F. Remove stem and seed core of each pepper. Cut each pepper in half lengthwise, place in shallow baking dish, drizzle with 1 tablespoon olive oil; toss to coat. Arrange peppers, cut side down, in single layer. Bake 15 to 20 minutes or until skins blister (not black). Remove from oven; let cool. Use your fingers or a sharp paring knife to pull off skins.

**To roast tomatoes, heat oven to 325°F. Cut off stem ends of tomatoes, place in shallow baking dish, drizzle with 2 tablespoons olive oil, season with salt and pepper. Roast 35 to 40 minutes, stirring every 15 minutes, until soft and just brown. Remove, let cool. Refrigerate until ready to use.

43

ACINI DI PEPE WITH CUCUMBERS, FETA AND GREEN PEPPERCORNS

This salad is particularly good served alongside roasted or grilled chicken, lamb or sausages.

1	tablespoon kosher (coarse) salt plus more to taste
8	oz. acini di pepe (peppercorn-shaped pasta)
4	tablespoons extra-virgin olive oil
1	small red onion, minced
1	cucumber, seeded, cut into 1/4-inch dice
3/4	cup feta cheese, crumbled (3 oz.)
2	teaspoons green peppercorns in brine, drained
12 to 16	fresh mint leaves, cut into very thin strips
12 to 16	fresh basil leaves, cut into very thin strips
	Freshly ground pepper to taste
3	tablespoons red wine vinegar
4 to 6	large romaine or butter lettuce leaves
6	mint or basil sprigs

❶ Fill large pot two-thirds full of water; add 1 tablespoon salt. Bring to a boil over high heat. Cook acini de pepe according to package directions; drain. Rinse thoroughly in cool water and drain. Transfer to medium bowl. Pour 2 tablespoons of the olive oil over pasta; toss gently to thoroughly coat.

❷ Toss onion, cucumber, cheese and peppercorns into pasta. Add mint and basil leaves; toss lightly. Season with salt and pepper.

❸ Pour vinegar and remaining 2 tablespoons olive oil over salad; toss again. Set aside 30 minutes. Place 1 lettuce leaf on each salad plate; spoon 3/4 to 1 cup salad onto each leaf. Garnish with mint and basil sprigs.

4 servings.

Preparation time: 20 minutes. Ready to serve: 1 hour.

Per serving: 470 calories, 25 g total fat (6 g saturated fat), 20 mg cholesterol, 790 mg sodium, 3 g fiber.

SMOKED FISH AND PASTA SALAD WITH FRIED SHALLOT MAYONNAISE

Spectrum Naturals, located in Petaluma, California, produces an exuberantly-flavored unrefined corn oil. The oil is delicate and unstable, so be sure you buy it in small amounts and use it quickly or it will go rancid.

    Fried Shallot Mayonnaise (recipe follows)
1   tablespoon kosher (coarse) salt plus more to taste
8   oz. torchio (torch-shaped pasta) or capanelli (flower-shaped pasta)
1/4 cup unrefined corn oil or mild olive oil
3   tablespoons capers, thoroughly drained
8   oz. smoked trout, smoked salmon or other dry-smoked fish fillet
3   scallions, trimmed, very thinly sliced
1   cup fresh corn kernels, cooked
1   tablespoon rice wine vinegar
    Freshly ground pepper to taste
4   hard-cooked eggs, peeled, cut into wedges
1/3 cup fried shallots (see Fried Shallot Mayonnaise)

❶ Prepare Fried Shallot Mayonnaise; set aside.

❷ Fill large pot two-thirds full of water; add 1 tablespoon salt. Bring to a boil over high heat. Cook torchio according to package directions; drain. Rinse and drain thoroughly in cool water. Transfer pasta to large bowl; drizzle with 1 tablespoon of the oil; toss gently.

❸ In small nonstick skillet, toast capers over medium heat 3 to 4 minutes, tossing frequently, until completely dry. Transfer to small bowl to cool.

❹ Break fish into bite-size pieces; add to pasta. Set aside 1 tablespoon of the scallions; add remaining scallions and corn to pasta and toss gently. Drizzle with remaining 3 tablespoons oil and vinegar. Add toasted capers; season with salt and pepper. Toss gently.

❺ Divide pasta evenly among 4 serving plates; garnish each with 4 wedges of hard-cooked egg. Top each egg wedge with 1/2 teaspoon mayonnaise.

Spoon 1 teaspoon mayonnaise on salad. Garnish with remaining scallions; sprinkle with reserved fried shallots.

4 servings.

Preparation time: 30 minutes. Ready to serve: 40 minutes.

Per serving: 665 calories, 38 g total fat (6 g saturated fat), 230 mg cholesterol, 1270 mg sodium, 4 g fiber.

FRIED SHALLOT MAYONNAISE

2   cups unrefined corn oil
3   medium shallots, very thinly sliced (about 2/3 cup)
1   pasteurized egg
2/3   cup olive oil
3   teaspoons rice wine vinegar
1/2   teaspoon sugar
    Kosher (coarse) salt to taste
    Freshly ground pepper to taste

❶ Heat corn oil in large skillet over medium heat to 350°F. Add shallots; cook, stirring constantly with wooden spoon until golden brown and crisp, about 3 minutes. Using a slotted spoon or long-handled strainer, transfer shallots to paper towels. Reserve about two-thirds of the fried shallots for salad garnish.

❷ Place remaining one-third fried shallots in mortar and pestle; grind into paste using pestle. Add egg; stir together thoroughly. Add olive oil, a few drops at a time, mixing with pestle. Continue until mixture has thickened. Fold in vinegar and sugar; season with salt and pepper. Cover and refrigerate.

2 3/4 cups.

Preparation time: 20 minutes. Ready to serve: 25 minutes.

Per serving (1 tablespoon): 120 calories, 13 g total fat (2 g saturated fat), 5 mg cholesterol, 80 mg sodium, 0 g fiber.

ORZO WITH SUMMER SQUASH CONFETTI, BASIL AND OLIVE OIL

The smaller the zucchini, the higher the ratio of peel, where much of the flavor is concentrated. You can make this using all green zucchini, but the yellow one will add a beautiful flash of color.

1	tablespoon kosher (coarse) salt plus more to taste
8	oz. orzo (rice-shaped pasta)
1	(5-inch) green zucchini, cut into 1/4-inch dice
1	(5-inch) crookneck squash or yellow zucchini, cut into 1/4-inch dice
3	small plum tomatoes, peeled, seeded, cut into 1/4-inch dice
1/3	cup red onion, minced
2	garlic cloves, minced
1	tablespoon fresh lemon juice
	Freshly ground pepper to taste
1/3	cup extra-virgin olive oil
12 to 15	fresh basil leaves, cut into very thin strips
6	small basil sprigs

❶ Fill large pot two-thirds full of water; add 1 tablespoon salt. Bring to a boil over high heat. Cook orzo according to package directions; drain. Rinse thoroughly in cool water and drain.

❷ Meanwhile, combine zucchini, crookneck squash, tomatoes, onion and garlic in medium bowl; add lemon juice. Season with salt and pepper; set aside.

❸ Add pasta to vegetables. Drizzle with olive oil; toss thoroughly. Add basil and toss gently. Garnish with basil sprigs.

4 servings.

Preparation time: 15 minutes. Ready to serve: 25 minutes.

Per serving: 400 calories, 20 g total fat (2 g saturated fat), 0 mg cholesterol, 520 mg sodium, 3.5 g fiber.

CHILLED SHELLFISH SALAD

Here the shellfish is chilled and the pasta is tossed with the chilled cooking juices, but the pasta itself is not chilled. It takes no extra effort to make the salad this way, and the results are much better than if you chilled the entire salad.

- 3 lbs. small hardshell Manila clams in the shell, thoroughly scrubbed*
- 3 lbs. Prince Edward Island mussels, thoroughly scrubbed
- 1 cup white wine
- 3 tablespoons olive oil
- 1/2 lb. small squid, thoroughly cleaned, peeled, tentacles and bodies separated
- 1/2 lb. bay shrimp, cooked
- 1/2 lb. fresh Dungeness crab meat, cooked
- Toasted Garlic Vinaigrette (recipe follows)
- 1 tablespoon kosher (coarse) salt plus more to taste
- 1 lb. lumache (shell-shaped pasta)
- 4 tablespoons minced fresh Italian parsley
- Freshly ground pepper to taste

❶ Place clams, mussels and wine in large pot. Heat to boiling. Cover; cook 6 to 7 minutes or until clam and mussel shells are open. Using slotted spoon, transfer mussels and clams to large, shallow bowl; let cool to room temperature, about 15 minutes.

❷ In medium skillet, heat olive oil over medium-high heat until hot. Add squid; sauté about 3 minutes, tossing frequently, until squid just turns opaque. Add squid, shrimp and crab to mussels and clams. Toss gently.

❸ Prepare Toasted Garlic Vinaigrette. Pour one-half of the vinaigrette over shellfish. Cover and refrigerate 1 hour.

❹ Fill another large pot two-thirds full of water; add 1 tablespoon salt. Bring to a boil over high heat. Cook lumache according to package directions; drain. Rinse and drain thoroughly in cool water. Transfer pasta to large bowl; toss with remaining vinaigrette. Toss, cover and set aside.

❺ Remove shellfish from refrigerator. Add pasta; toss gently but thoroughly. Add parsley, toss lightly; season with salt and pepper.

8 servings.
Preparation time: 1 hour, 20 minutes. Ready to serve: 3 hours, 30 minutes (includes chilling time).

Per serving: 955 calories, 55 g total fat (8 g saturated fat), 250 mg cholesterol, 980 mg sodium, 3 g fiber.

TIP *Clams and mussels can be removed from their shells after they are cooked.

TOASTED GARLIC VINAIGRETTE

    6   garlic cloves, very thinly sliced
  1/4   cup champagne or white wine vinegar
    2   teaspoons grated lemon peel
  1/3   cup fresh lemon juice
    1   teaspoon kosher (coarse) salt
        Freshly ground pepper to taste
1 1/4   cups extra-virgin olive oil

❶ Toast garlic in medium skillet over medium-low heat, tossing frequently, until garlic is lightly browned and just crisp, about 10 minutes. Set aside to cool.

❷ In medium bowl, whisk together vinegar, lemon peel and lemon juice. Season with salt and pepper; whisk in olive oil. Gently stir in toasted garlic.

1 2/3 cups.
Preparation time: 20 minutes. Ready to serve: 20 minutes.

Per serving: 175 calories, 20 g total fat (3 g saturated fat), 0 mg cholesterol, 115 mg sodium, 0 g fiber.

A simple loaf of fresh Italian bread contrasts wonderfully with the complex textures of Chilled Shellfish Salad.

WARM TAGLIATELLE SALAD WITH GRILLED FIGS, PROSCIUTTO, ARUGULA AND BLACK PEPPER

Add three-quarters of a teaspoon of freshly ground pepper to the pasta flour. It will add an appealing jolt of heat — a sultry sort of bass note — to this dish.

1 tablespoon kosher (coarse) salt plus more to taste

6 black figs, cut in half lengthwise

4 tablespoons extra-virgin olive oil

1 recipe *One Egg Pasta* (page 11) with 3/4 teaspoon freshly ground pepper, cut into tagliatelle

3 oz. prosciutto, 1/8-inch thick, cut into 1/2-inch crosswise strips

2 tablespoons balsamic vinegar

Freshly ground pepper to taste

3 cups young arugula

❶ Heat grill. Bring 2 quarts water to a boil; add 1 tablespoon salt.

❷ Meanwhile, use pastry brush to coat cut surfaces of figs with 1 tablespoon of the olive oil. Place figs, cut side down, on gas grill over medium heat or on charcoal grill 4 to 6 inches from medium coals. Cook 5 to 7 minutes or until hot. Transfer to plate.

❸ Cook pasta in boiling water about 2 minutes or until just done; drain. Rinse thoroughly in cool water and drain. Transfer pasta to medium bowl; add prosciutto. Drizzle with 1 1/2 tablespoons olive oil and 1 tablespoon of the balsamic vinegar. Season with salt and pepper. Set aside.

❹ Place arugula in large bowl. Season with salt; toss. Drizzle with remaining 1 1/2 tablespoons olive oil and remaining 1 tablespoon balsamic vinegar; toss again. Divide arugula evenly among salad plates. Top each portion with 1 cup pasta and prosciutto. Divide grilled figs among plates; season with pepper.

4 servings.

Preparation time: 45 minutes. Ready to serve: 55 minutes.

Per serving: 365 calories, 18 g total fat (4 g saturated fat), 65 mg cholesterol, 900 mg sodium, 4 g fiber.

ARTICHOKE, CHICKEN AND PASTA SALAD

Fresh artichokes have a nutty, earthy flavor and texture — something quite different from those you find in a can or jar, which taste primarily of the brine or vinegar in which they are preserved.

1	tablespoon kosher (coarse) salt plus more to taste
8	oz. capanelle (flower-shaped pasta)
1	shallot, minced
2 1/2	tablespoons fresh lemon juice
	Freshly ground pepper to taste
2	teaspoons minced fresh tarragon or 1 teaspoon dried beaux herbs
1/4	cup extra-virgin olive oil
2	fresh artichoke hearts, cooked, thinly sliced
1/2	cup cracked green olives, pitted, sliced
1	cup cooked shredded dark chicken meat

❶ Fill large pot two-thirds full of water; add 1 tablespoon salt. Bring to a boil over high heat. Cook capanelle according to package directions; drain. Rinse and drain thoroughly in cool water. Transfer pasta to shallow bowl.

❷ Meanwhile, in small bowl, cover shallot with lemon juice. Season with salt, pepper and 2 teaspoons tarragon; whisk in olive oil.

❸ Add artichoke hearts, olives and chicken to cooked pasta. Pour dressing over pasta and vegetables; toss gently but thoroughly.

4 servings.
Preparation time: 15 minutes.
Ready to serve: 30 minutes.

Per serving: 490 calories, 26 g total fat (4 g saturated fat), 30 mg cholesterol, 1010 mg sodium, 4 g fiber.

ROASTED BEET AND PASTA SALAD WITH ORANGE VINAIGRETTE

When you want something light and delicate in the winter, this salad's orange juice provides a bright burst of flavor while beets, roasted in the oven, contribute an appealingly sweet flourish.

4	medium beets, preferably golden or Chioggia
1	tablespoon olive oil
1	tablespoon kosher (coarse) salt plus more to taste
12	oz. small tube-shaped pasta, such as elbow macaroni
1	small shallot, minced
1	tablespoon champagne vinegar
1/3	cup freshly squeezed orange juice
	Zest of 1 orange, grated
1/2	cup walnut oil
2	thin slices prosciutto*
1/2	cup feta cheese, crumbled (2 oz.)
12	Kalamata olives, pitted, sliced
1/2	cup walnut pieces, lightly toasted
3	tablespoons minced fresh Italian parsley

❶ Heat oven to 350°F. Wash and trim beets; do not peel.

❷ Set beets in 1-quart casserole; toss with olive oil. Roast until tender when pierced with fork, about 40 minutes. Remove from oven; let cool. Peel beets; cut into medium dice. Place diced beets into large bowl.

❸ Fill medium pot two-thirds full of water; add 1 tablespoon salt. Bring to a boil over high heat. Cook pasta until *al dente*; drain. Rinse and drain thoroughly in cool water. Combine pasta with beets. Set aside.

❹ Meanwhile, prepare vinaigrette. Place shallot in small bowl; pour vinegar over shallot. Marinate 15 minutes. Stir in orange juice; season with salt. Whisk in walnut oil; set aside. Add prosciutto, cheese, olives and walnuts to pasta and beets; toss gently. Pour vinaigrette over pasta; toss again. Sprinkle with Italian parsley.

4 servings.

Preparation time: 20 minutes. Ready to serve: 50 minutes.

Per serving: 755 calories, 42 g total fat (6 g saturated fat), 15 mg cholesterol, 690 mg sodium, 5.5g fiber.

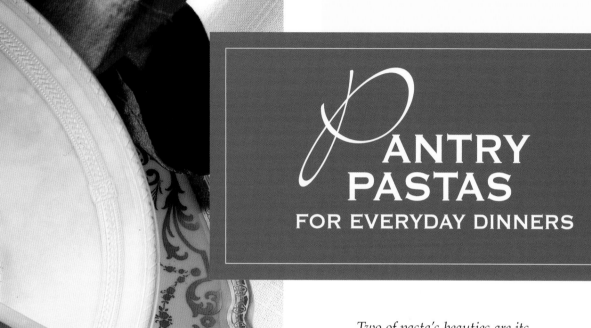

PANTRY PASTAS

FOR EVERYDAY DINNERS

Two of pasta's beauties are its simplicity and versatility. Stock a few basic items in your pantry and you are prepared to make a variety of great pasta meals on the fly. Here are the ingredients, and the recipes, you'll need.

Fettuccine with Dried Tomato Tapenade, page 72

STOCKING THE PANTRY

If you have a well-stocked pantry, you should be able to make any of the pasta recipes that follow without a trip to the market. A basic pantry should include:

IN THE CUPBOARD

Anchovies packed in oil

Bread crumbs (homemade)

Canned beef broth

Canned chicken broth

Canned crushed tomatoes

Canned diced tomatoes

Canned tuna

Capers

Cayenne pepper

Crushed red pepper

Dried pastas

Dried tomato tapenade or concentrated purée

Dry red wine

Dry white wine

Extra-virgin olive oil

Fresh lemons

Freshly ground pepper

Garlic, fresh (not sprouted)

Honey

Kosher (coarse) salt

Olive oil for cooking

Olive tapenade

Potatoes (stored separately, away from onions and garlic)

Sardines packed in oil

Single malt scotch

Vinegars: white wine or champagne; sherry; commercial balsamic; red wine

Yellow onions

IN THE REFRIGERATOR

Butter

Cheeses: dry Jack, Parmigiano-Reggiano, Asiago, Gorgonzola

Cream

Eggs

Half-and-half

Italian parsley, stored in water, in a wide-mouth jar with a plastic bag fitted loosely over the top

Pancetta (store in the freezer if you don't use it very often)

Walnuts

IN THE FREEZER

Butter

Smoked salmon

Stocks: chicken, meat, vegetable (homemade)

IN THE GARDEN

It is also helpful to grow a few herbs in your garden or even in a small clay pot. You'll want chives, oregano, rosemary and thyme.

STROZZAPRETI WITH GARLIC AND PANCETTA

Strozzapreti means "priest choker", a name that refers to the rope-like shape of this handmade pasta. If unavailable, try this dish with pasta shapes such as gemelli (double twists), al ceppo (2-inch rolled tubes) or garganelli (hand-rolled tubes using fresh egg pasta).

1   tablespoon kosher (coarse) salt plus more to taste
1   (8.8-oz.) pkg. strozzapreti or other medium-length pasta
1/2 teaspoon olive oil
3   oz. pancetta, diced
6   garlic cloves, minced
1/2 teaspoon chipotle flakes or crushed red pepper
3   tablespoons extra-virgin olive oil
2   tablespoons minced fresh Italian parsley
    Freshly ground pepper to taste
1   block Parmigiano-Reggiano cheese (3 oz.)

❶ Fill large pot two-thirds full of water; add 1 tablespoon salt. Bring to a boil over high heat. Cook strozzapretti according to package directions; drain. Transfer to warm serving bowl.

❷ Meanwhile, heat olive oil in small skillet over medium-low heat until hot; fry pancetta about 7 minutes or until almost crispy. Add garlic and chipotle flakes; sauté until garlic is fragrant and very lightly browned, about 2 minutes. Remove mixture from heat; cool slightly. Add extra-virgin olive oil.

❸ Pour pancetta mixture over pasta; toss gently but thoroughly. Season with 2 tablespoons parsley, salt and pepper; toss gently. Grate cheese over pasta. Divide pasta evenly among plates. Pass cheese and grater along with pasta.

4 servings.

Preparation time: 5 minutes. Ready to serve: 20 minutes.

Per serving: 1040 calories, 69 g total fat (19 g saturated fat), 150 mg cholesterol, 1060 mg sodium, 4 g fiber.

SPAGHETTI WITH GARLIC AND OLIVE OIL

If you assemble all the ingredients while the water boils, dinner will be ready in the amount of time it takes to cook the pasta!

1	tablespoon kosher (coarse) salt plus more to taste
12	oz. dried spaghetti or other thin pasta strand
2	tablespoons olive oil
4 to 6	garlic cloves, minced
1/2	teaspoon chipotle flakes or crushed red pepper
1/3	cup extra-virgin olive oil
1	tablespoon minced fresh Italian parsley
1	teaspoon minced fresh oregano leaves
1	teaspoon minced fresh thyme leaves
	Freshly ground pepper to taste

❶ Fill large pot two-thirds full of water; add 1 tablespoon salt. Bring to a boil over high heat. Cook spaghetti according to package directions; drain. Transfer to shallow serving bowl.

❷ Meanwhile, heat 2 tablespoons olive oil in small skillet over medium-low heat; add garlic and simmer gently 3 minutes or until it just begins to soften. Add chipotle flakes; remove from heat. Set aside.

❸ Add extra-virgin olive oil to garlic mixture; pour over pasta. Add parsley, oregano and thyme. Season with salt and pepper; toss gently. Divide pasta evenly among plates. Pass Parmigiano-Reggiano or dry jack cheese and grater along with the pasta, if desired.

4 servings.

Preparation time: 10 minutes. Ready to serve: 20 minutes.

Per serving: 500 calories, 26 g total fat (4 g saturated fat), 0 mg cholesterol, 575 mg sodium, 3 g fiber.

ETTUCCINE WITH GORGONZOLA AND WALNUTS

Walnuts are harvested in the early fall; the best are dried in the sun before they go to market. Store walnuts in the refrigerator.

1   cup whipping cream
2   garlic cloves, minced
3   tablespoons minced fresh Italian parsley
1/2   cup toasted walnuts, chopped
1   tablespoon kosher (coarse) salt plus more to taste
    Freshly ground pepper to taste
1   recipe *Two-Egg Pasta* (page 12), cut into fettuccine
1   cup grated Gorgonzola cheese (4 oz.)

❶ In medium saucepan over medium heat, simmer cream about 10 minutes or until reduced by one-third; stir often. In small bowl, combine garlic, parsley and walnuts. Season with salt and pepper; set aside.

❷ Fill large pot two-thirds full of water; add 1 tablespoon salt. Bring to a boil over high heat. Cook fettuccine in boiling water 1 1/2 to 2 minutes or until tender. Do not overcook. Drain pasta; transfer to shallow serving bowl.

❸ Meanwhile, reheat cream until hot; stir in 1 cup Gorgonzola and pepper to taste. Remove from heat. Pour sauce over pasta; toss until evenly coated. Divide among serving plates. Sprinkle walnut mixture over each portion.

4 servings.

Preparation time: 45 minutes. Ready to serve: 15 minutes.

Per serving: 510 calories, 37.5 g total fat (18 g saturated fat), 140 mg cholesterol, 825 mg sodium, 2 g fiber.

SPAGHETTI MARINARA

Leftover spaghetti marinara is a real treat. Try it cold for breakfast, or hot anytime at all.

2	tablespoons olive oil
1	small yellow onion, diced
3 to 4	garlic cloves, minced
2	tablespoons kosher (coarse) salt plus more to taste
2	teaspoons dried oregano
1/2	teaspoon dried thyme
1/4	teaspoon crushed red pepper plus more to taste
3/4	cup red wine, if desired
2	(28-oz.) cans crushed or chopped tomatoes
2	tablespoons tomato paste, if desired
1 1/2	lbs. dried spaghettini or spaghetti
1	block Parmigiano or dry Monterey Jack cheese (3 oz.)

❶ Heat olive oil in heavy skillet over medium-low heat until hot. Add onion; sauté 4 minutes or until soft and fragrant. Add garlic; sauté an additional 2 minutes. Season with salt, 2 teaspoons oregano, 1/2 teaspoon thyme and 1/4 teaspoon crushed red pepper. Increase heat to high; stir in wine. Simmer over high heat until wine is reduced by two-thirds, about 4 minutes. Stir in tomatoes and tomato paste. Reduce heat to medium; simmer 15 minutes or until sauce is slightly thickened.

❷ Fill large pot two-thirds full of water; add 1 tablespoon salt. Bring to a boil over high heat. Cook spaghetti according to package directions; drain. Transfer to large bowl.

❸ Pour sauce over pasta; toss thoroughly. Divide pasta evenly among plates. Pass cheese and grater and shaker of crushed red pepper with pasta.

6 to 8 servings.
Preparation time: 10 minutes. Ready to serve: 35 minutes.
Per serving: 840 calories, 12 g total fat (2 g saturated fat), 2 mg cholesterol, 1660 mg sodium, 11 g fiber.

EGG PASTA WITH BUTTER, BLACK PEPPER AND AGED ASIAGO

Pastas made with eggs are more tender and delicate than those made with just water and wheat. You want to keep a few packages of good commercial egg pasta on hand to use when you're really busy.

1   tablespoon kosher (coarse) salt plus more to taste
1   recipe *One-Egg Pasta* (page 11), cut into fettuccine or tagliatelle
4   tablespoons organic butter, softened
    Freshly ground pepper to taste
1   block aged Asiago cheese (3 oz.)

❶ Fill large pot two-thirds full of water to a boil; add 1 tablespoon salt. Bring to a boil over high heat. Cook pasta about 1½ minutes or until tender, being careful not to overcook; drain.

❷ Transfer pasta to warmed serving bowl. Add butter; toss gently until butter is melted. Season with salt and pepper. Divide pasta evenly among plates; grate Asiago over each portion.

4 servings.
Preparation time: 5 minutes. Ready to serve: 15 minutes.

Per serving: 330 calories, 18 g total fat (10 g saturated fat), 115 mg cholesterol, 790 mg sodium, 1 g fiber.

PASTA WITH SMOKED SALMON, SCOTCH, CREAM AND CAPERS

If you grow your own chives you probably have chive flowers much of the year. If so, this is a great place to use them. You can use smoked trout or another smoked fish in its place if you don't have smoked salmon.

1	tablespoon kosher (coarse) salt
8.8	oz. cencioni or 10 oz. papardelle
3/4	cup single-malt Scotch
1	cup whipping cream
6	oz. dry-smoked salmon, broken into bite-size pieces
2	tablespoons fresh-snipped chives
	Freshly ground pepper to taste
2	tablespoons pickled capers, drained
3	chives flowers, individual flowers separated, if desired

❶ Fill large pot two-thirds full of water; add 1 tablespoon salt. Bring to a boil over high heat. Cook cencioni according to package directions; drain. Transfer to shallow bowl.

❷ Meanwhile, heat Scotch in small saucepan over high heat; boil until reduced to 1/4 cup. Reduce heat to medium-low. Add cream; simmer about 5 minutes or until reduced by one-third. Stir in salmon and chives. Season with pepper; remove from heat.

❸ Toast capers in small, nonstick skillet over medium heat, tossing frequently, 3 to 4 minutes or until completely dry. Transfer to small bowl to cool.

❹ Pour salmon mixture over pasta; toss gently until pasta is thoroughly coated. Divide among bowls or plates; sprinkle with capers and chive flowers.

4 servings.

Preparation time: 10 minutes. Ready to serve: 25 minutes.

Per serving: 625 calories, 29 g total fat (16 g saturated fat), 100 mg cholesterol, 950 mg sodium, 3 g fiber.

SIMPLE FIDEOS (FRIED CATALAN-STYLE PASTA) WITH LEMON SAUCE

There are dozens of versions of this Catalan pasta dish in northeastern Spain. Some are this simple; others are as complex as a paella, but made with noodles instead of rice.

2	garlic cloves, crushed
	Kosher (coarse) salt to taste
1	pasteurized egg yolk
2	tablespoons grated lemon peel
2/3	cup extra-virgin olive oil
1/4	cup lemon juice
1	tablespoon olive oil
10	oz. fideos or other thin pasta, such as spaghettini, broken into 1-inch pieces
1 1/2	cups hot *Chicken Stock* (page 22)
1 1/2	cups hot water

❶ Place garlic cloves in food processor; sprinkle with salt and grind garlic to paste. Add egg yolk and lemon peel; mix together thoroughly until garlic and egg yolk are completely smooth. Mix in olive oil, a few drops at a time, and continue until oil is incorporated. Add lemon juice; add more salt if necessary. Cover and set aside.

❷ Heat olive oil in large skillet over medium-low heat until hot; add pasta and cook, stirring constantly, until pasta is golden brown, about 12 minutes. Season with salt; add 1/2 cup of the Chicken Stock. Continue to stir as pasta cooks in stock. When pasta has absorbed stock, add another 1/2 cup, stirring until absorbed. Add remaining 1/2 cup stock; continue stirring.

❸ Add water as needed, 1/4 cup at a time, stirring constantly about 12 minutes or until al dente. Season to taste; divide among plates, top with spoonful of lemon sauce, and serve immediately with remaining lemon sauce.

4 servings.

Preparation time: 10 minutes. Ready to serve: 40 minutes.

Per serving: 880 calories, 57 g total fat (8 g saturated fat), 70 mg cholesterol, 700 mg sodium, 4 g fiber.

FUSILLI LUNGHI WITH TUNA SAUCE

Turn a can of tuna into a wonderful pasta sauce.

 1 tablespoon kosher (coarse) salt
12 oz. fusilli lunghi or fusilli col buco (spiral-shaped pasta)
 1 tablespoon olive oil
 6 garlic cloves, minced
 4 anchovy fillets, minced
 2 teaspoons grated lemon peel
 1 (6$\frac{1}{2}$-oz.) can tuna in olive oil
$\frac{1}{4}$ cup dry white wine
$\frac{1}{4}$ cup fresh lemon juice
$\frac{1}{4}$ cup minced fresh Italian parsley
$\frac{1}{4}$ cup minced kalamata olives
$\frac{1}{2}$ teaspoon crushed red pepper
   Freshly ground pepper to taste
$\frac{3}{4}$ cup fresh bread crumbs, toasted

❶ Fill large pot two-thirds full of water; add 1 tablespoon salt. Bring to a boil over high heat. Cook fusilli according to package directions; drain. Do not rinse.

❷ Meanwhile, heat olive oil in medium skillet over medium heat until hot; add garlic and anchovies. Sauté until garlic just begins to turn color and anchovies nearly dissolve. Add lemon peel, tuna, wine, lemon juice, parsley, olives and crushed red pepper. Use fork to break up tuna; simmer 4 minutes or until tuna is hot. Season with pepper; remove from heat.

❸ Place cooked pasta in shallow bowl; pour sauce over pasta. Toss thoroughly. Sprinkle bread crumbs over pasta. Divide pasta evenly among plates.

4 servings.
Preparation time: 10 minutes. Ready to serve: 25 minutes.

Per serving: 660 calories, 22.5 g total fat (3.5 g saturated fat), 10 mg cholesterol, 880 mg sodium, 4.5 g fiber.

ROSAMARINA WITH COMPOUND BUTTER

This pasta makes an excellent side dish when served with roasted or grilled meats and vegetables. It can also be a building block for more complex recipes. Or serve it as a simple first or main course on a busy night. Use the Basic Compound Butter recipe and one of the 5 variations provided.

1 tablespoon kosher (coarse) salt, plus more to taste
8 oz. rosamarina, semi di melone or other small seed-shaped pasta
3 tablespoons Compound Butter, cut into pieces (recipes follow)
  Freshly ground pepper to taste

❶ Fill large pot two-thirds full of water; add 1 tablespoon salt. Bring to a boil over high heat. Cook rosamarina according to package directions; drain. Transfer to warm serving bowl.

❷ Add compound butter; toss until melted. Season with salt and pepper. Divide pasta evenly among plates.

4 servings.
Preparation time: 15 minutes. Ready to serve: 20 minutes.

Per serving: 270 calories, 7 g total fat (4 g saturated fat), 15 mg cholesterol, 515 mg sodium, 2 g fiber.

BASIC COMPOUND BUTTER

1/2 cup unsalted butter, softened
  Seasoning (see variations below)
1/2 teaspoon kosher (coarse) salt
1/2 teaspoon freshly ground pepper

❶ Place butter in food processor; add seasoning (choices below), salt and pepper. Pulse until butter and seasoning are evenly mixed. Transfer to small crock or onto sheet of parchment paper. Shape into log about 1 1/4 inches in diameter. Roll parchment around butter; roll butter package in plastic wrap. Refrigerate up to 5 days or freeze up to 3 weeks.

Preparation time: 15 minutes. Ready to serve: 20 minutes.

CILANTRO BUTTER SEASONING

3 tablespoons minced fresh cilantro

1 serrano chile

1 teaspoon grated lime peel

Per 1 tablespoon serving: 70 calories, 8 g total fat (4.5 g saturated fat), 20 mg cholesterol, 0 mg sodium, 0 g fiber.

GARLIC-HERB BUTTER SEASONING

2 garlic cloves, crushed

3 tablespoons minced fresh herbs, such as oregano, Italian parsley, chives, thyme or rosemary

Per 1 tablespoon serving: 70 calories, 8 g total fat (4.5 g saturated fat), 20 mg cholesterol, 0 mg sodium, 0 g fiber.

GORGONZOLA BUTTER SEASONING

3 oz. Italian Gorgonzola cheese

1 tablespoon minced fresh Italian parsley

Per 1 tablespoon serving: 75 calories, 8 g total fat (5 g saturated fat), 20 mg cholesterol, 80 mg sodium, 0 g fiber.

LEMON BUTTER SEASONING

3 tablespoons minced lemon peel

1 tablespoon minced fresh Italian parsley

2 garlic cloves, crushed

Per 1 tablespoon serving: 70 calories, 8 g total fat (5 g saturated fat), 20 mg cholesterol, 0 mg sodium, 0 g fiber.

OLIVE BUTTER SEASONING

1 garlic clove, crushed

1/2 small shallot

2 tablespoons minced oil-cured olives

1 teaspoon fresh thyme leaves

Per 1 tablespoon serving: 70 calories, 8 g total fat (5 g saturated fat), 20 mg cholesterol, 15 mg sodium, 0 g fiber.

FETTUCCINE WITH DRIED TOMATO TAPENADE

Dried tomatoes are best used in the winter months when their concentrated flavor keeps you warm against a cold night. You can find dried tomato puree in tubes, easy to keep in the refrigerator for this quick — but delicious — pasta dish.

- 1 tablespoon kosher (coarse) salt
- 1 10 to 12 oz. dried fettuccine
- 1 cup whipping cream
- 1/3 cup prepared tapenade
- Freshly ground pepper to taste
- 2 tablespoons minced fresh Italian parsley
- 1/2 cup freshly grated dry Monterey Jack or Parmigiano-Reggiano cheese (2 oz.)

1 Fill large pot two-thirds full of water; add 1 tablespoon salt. Bring to a boil over high heat. Cook fettuccine according to package directions; drain. Do not rinse.

2 Meanwhile, heat cream to a boil in small saucepan over medium heat. Reduce heat; simmer about 8 minutes or until reduced by one-third. Stir tapenade into cream. Remove from heat.

3 Place cooked pasta in shallow bowl; pour sauce over pasta and toss to coat thoroughly. Season with pepper, 2 tablespoons parsley and 1/2 cup cheese; toss lightly. Divide pasta evenly among plates.

4 servings.
Preparation time: 10 minutes.
Ready to serve: 20 minutes.

Per serving: 575 calories, 35 g total fat (15 g saturated fat), 135 mg cholesterol, 730 mg sodium, 4 g fiber.

SPAGHETTI WITH TAPENADE

If you have a jar of commercial tapenade and a package of spaghetti in the cupboard, you're in business. If you have fresh herbs, either in the refrigerator or in the garden, so much the better! If you have a harvest of cherry tomatoes, slice enough to make 2 cups; toss with pasta when adding herbs.

1	tablespoon kosher (coarse) salt plus more to taste
8 to 10	oz. dried spaghettini or other thin pasta strand
1/3	cup prepared tapenade
3	tablespoons extra-virgin olive oil
2 to 3	garlic cloves, pressed
3	tablespoons minced fresh herbs, such as Italian parsley, oregano, marjoram, thyme, basil or chives
	Freshly ground pepper to taste

❶ Fill large pot two-thirds full of water; add 1 tablespoon salt. Bring to a boil over high heat. Cook spaghettini according to package directions; drain. Do not rinse.

❷ Meanwhile, in small bowl, stir together tapenade, olive oil and garlic. Place pasta in shallow bowl. Spoon tapenade mixture over pasta; toss thoroughly. Add 3 tablespoons herbs; season with salt and pepper. Toss again. Divide pasta evenly among plates.

3 to 4 servings.
Preparation time: 10 minutes.
Ready to serve: 20 minutes.

Per serving: 550 calories, 28 g total fat (4 g saturated fat), 0 mg cholesterol, 820 mg sodium, 5 g fiber.

SPAGHETTI WITH GARLIC, ANCHOVIES, CAPERS AND BREAD CRUMBS

Look for salted capers in the deli sections of good markets. If you can't find them, use brined ones. When you have leftover bread, save it to make bread crumbs. If you use pickled capers, rinse them in water and toast gently in a dry pan.

1	tablespoon kosher (coarse) salt plus more to taste
1	10 to 12 oz. dried spaghetti
1/4	cup olive oil
6	garlic cloves, minced
8	anchovy fillets, drained, minced
1/2	teaspoon crushed red pepper
1/3	cup extra-virgin olive oil
2	tablespoons salted capers
	Freshly ground pepper to taste
2	teaspoons minced fresh oregano
2	tablespoons minced fresh Italian parsley
1/2	cup coarse fresh bread crumbs, lightly toasted

❶ Fill large pot two-thirds full of water; add 1 tablespoon salt. Bring to a boil over high heat. Cook pasta according to package directions; drain. Transfer to warm serving bowl.

❷ Meanwhile, heat 2 tablespoons of the olive oil in small skillet over medium-low heat; add garlic and sauté about 2 minutes or until soft and fragrant. Stir in anchovies and sauté an additional 2 minutes while anchovies dissolve. Stir in crushed red pepper; remove from heat. Add remaining 2 tablespoons olive oil and capers; set aside.

❸ Pour olive oil mixture over pasta; toss thoroughly. Season with salt and pepper, oregano, parsley and one-half of the bread crumbs; toss thoroughly. Sprinkle remaining bread crumbs over pasta.

4 servings.

Preparation time: 10 minutes. Ready to serve: 25 minutes.

Per serving: 570 calories, 27 g total fat (4 g saturated fat), 5 mg cholesterol, 950 mg sodium, 4 g fiber.

$\mathcal{E}$ASY PASTA DISHES
FOR WEEKDAY DINNERS

These pastas rely primarily upon the pantry, but may require a quick trip to the grocery store or farmers' market for fresh vegetables and a few other perishable ingredients you may not have on hand. But they require about the same amount of work as those in the Pantry Pastas chapter, which is to say, not a whole lot. In each, the most important ingredient is a good pasta.

Cherry Tomatoes, Parsley, Garlic, Olive Oil and Gnocchi, page 89

PENNE WITH ASPARAGUS AND TOASTED HAZELNUTS

Once you have roasted asparagus you'll never again return to boiling or steaming it. Roasting intensifies the flavors and, as an added bonus, eliminates the need to peel it — even the larger spears. It's also a very easy technique.

2   tablespoons olive oil
1   lb. asparagus spears, tough ends removed, cut into 2-inch lengths
1   tablespoon kosher (coarse) salt plus more to taste
    Freshly ground pepper to taste
12 oz. trenne or penne (tube-shaped pasta)
2   tablespoons *Clarified Butter* (page 18)
1   cup shredded or grated smoked mozzarella (4 oz.)
1/2 cup shelled hazelnuts, toasted, skinned, coarsely chopped

❶ Heat oven to 450°F. In large bowl, toss 2 tablespoons olive oil with asparagus until evenly coated. Spread asparagus on 15x10-inch baking sheet in single layer; season with salt and pepper. Bake 7 to 10 minutes or until just tender. Remove from oven and let cool until easy to handle.

❷ Fill large pot two-thirds full of water; add 1 tablespoon salt. Bring to a boil over high heat. Cook trenne according to package directions; drain. Do not rinse. Transfer cooked pasta to serving bowl.

❸ Meanwhile, cut each piece of roasted asparagus in half lengthwise. Melt 2 tablespoons Clarified Butter in medium skillet over medium heat; add asparagus. Toss and cook until heated through. Pour cooked asparagus over pasta; add mozzarella. Toss gently but thoroughly. Divide pasta evenly among plates; top each portion with hazelnuts.

4 servings.

Preparation time: 20 minutes. Ready to serve: 30 minutes.

Per serving: 635 calories, 29 g total fat (10 g saturated fat), 40 mg cholesterol, 775 mg sodium, 5 g fiber.

GEMELLI WITH GREEN BEANS, WALNUTS, BACON AND GORGONZOLA

Depending on where you live, haricots verts — tiny green beans about as thick as a pencil — can be easy or impossible to find. If you can't get them, choose the smallest Blue Lake green beans you can find.

1	tablespoon kosher (coarse) salt plus more to taste
8 to 10	oz. gemelli, al ceppo or other medium-length pasta
4 to 6	slices bacon, cut into 1/2-inch-wide strips
3	tablespoons olive oil
1	shallot, minced
3	garlic cloves, minced
4	oz. haricots verts or very small Blue Lake green beans, blanched, drained
3/4	cup walnut pieces, toasted
3/4	cup imported Gorgonzola, broken into small pieces (3 oz.)
	Freshly ground pepper to taste

❶ Fill large pot two-thirds full of water; add 1 tablespoon salt. Bring to a boil over high heat. Cook gemelli according to package directions; drain. Do not rinse.

❷ Meanwhile, fry bacon in medium skillet until almost crisp. Transfer bacon to paper towels; discard bacon fat. Return pan to medium heat; add 1 1/2 tablespoons of the olive oil and shallot. Sauté 5 minutes or until shallot is soft and fragrant. Add garlic; sauté an additional two minutes. Add haricots verts and walnuts; toss thoroughly to heat through.

❸ Transfer pasta to shallow bowl; add green bean mixture and remaining 1 1/2 tablespoons olive oil. Toss thoroughly. Add Gorgonzola and bacon; toss again. Season with salt and pepper. Divide pasta evenly among plates.

4 servings.

Preparation time: 10 minutes. Ready to serve: 20 minutes.

Per serving: 560 calories, 32 g total fat (8 g saturated fat), 20 mg cholesterol, 925 mg sodium, 4 g fiber.

SUMMER PASTA WITH TOMATO AND BUTTER SAUCE

When you enrich a simple tomato sauce with butter, you round out the acidity and add a voluptuousness that is best paired with a broad pasta noodle such as fettuccine. Because of the delicacy of the sauce, it goes beautifully with fresh pasta too.

4	tablespoons unsalted butter
2	shallots, minced
2	lbs. plum tomatoes, peeled, seeded, diced
1	tablespoon kosher (coarse) salt plus more to taste
	Freshly ground pepper to taste
10 to 12	oz. fettuccine
2	tablespoons minced fresh chives or fresh Italian parsley
3/4	cup Parmigiano-Reggiano cheese (3 oz.)

❶ Heat 2 tablespoons of the butter in medium skillet over medium heat. When foamy, add shallots; sauté about 8 minutes or until soft and fragrant. Add tomatoes; cook until liquid in tomatoes is nearly evaporated. Season with salt and pepper; remove from heat and set aside.

❷ Fill large pot two-thirds full of water; add 1 tablespoon salt. Bring to a boil over high heat. Cook fettuccine according to package directions; drain. Do not rinse. Transfer cooked pasta to shallow bowl.

❸ Return tomato sauce to medium heat; heat through. Remove from heat. Swirl in remaining 2 tablespoons butter and chives. Pour sauce over hot pasta; toss gently. Divide pasta evenly among plates; grate cheese over each portion.

4 servings.

Preparation time: 20 minutes. Ready to serve: 35 minutes.

Per serving: 400 calories, 16 g total fat (8 g saturated fat), 95 mg cholesterol, 510 mg sodium, 5 g fiber.

SPAGHETTINI WITH PARSLEY SAUCE

In most versions of this traditional sauce, you'll find several anchovies. Feel free to add them when you add the walnuts and garlic. But if you find yourself cooking for people who don't care for anchovies, as I sometimes do, you'll appreciate this version.

1 tablespoon kosher (coarse) salt plus more to taste

1 lb. dried spaghettini

3 cups Italian parsley leaves

6 garlic cloves, minced

1/2 cup walnut pieces, toasted

2 tablespoons grated lemon peel

1/4 cup fresh lemon juice

2 teaspoons Dijon mustard

  Freshly ground pepper to taste

1/2 cup extra-virgin olive oil plus more to taste

1 tablespoon capers

❶ Fill large pot two-thirds full of water; add 1 tablespoon salt. Bring to a boil over high heat. Cook spaghettini according to package directions; drain. Do not rinse. Reserve about 1/4 cup cooking water.

❷ Meanwhile, process parsley, garlic, walnuts, lemon peel, lemon juice and mustard in food processor. Pulse several times, scraping sides of bowl with rubber spatula if necessary, until mixture is uniformly minced. Transfer to medium bowl; season with salt and pepper. Stir in olive oil and capers; taste. If sauce seems tart, add 2 to 3 tablespoons olive oil.

❸ Transfer cooked pasta to deep bowl; pour sauce over pasta. Add 2 tablespoons cooking water. Toss until pasta is evenly coated with sauce; if it seems too thick, add more cooking water and toss again. Divide pasta evenly among plates.

4 servings.

Preparation time: 30 minutes. Ready to serve: 35 minutes.

Per serving: 820 calories, 40 g total fat (5 g saturated fat), 0 mg cholesterol, 720 mg sodium, 7 g fiber.

PAPARDELLE WITH PROSCIUTTO, SPINACH AND CREAM

Spinach is best cooked very quickly so that it retains its fresh green flavors. Papardelle, a very broad noodle, is usually sold in half-pound packages, enough for a main course for two or three adults, or a first course for three or four people.

1	tablespoon kosher (coarse) salt plus more to taste
1	(8.8-oz.) pkg. papardelle
1 1/4	cups whipping cream
1	teaspoon freshly ground nutmeg plus more to taste
	Freshly ground pepper to taste
3	oz. prosciutto, sliced 1/16-inch thick
8	oz. young spinach leaves, washed
1/2	cup grated fresh Asiago cheese (2 oz.)

❶ Fill large pot two-thirds full of water; add 1 tablespoon salt. Bring to a boil over high heat. Cook papardelle according to package directions; drain. Do not rinse.

❷ Meanwhile, pour cream into medium saucepan; bring to a boil over medium heat. Stir often. Reduce heat to medium-low; simmer about 10 minutes or until reduced by one-third. Add nutmeg and season with pepper; set aside and keep hot. Cut prosciutto into thin crosswise strips; heat through in medium skillet over medium heat. Add spinach; cover and cook about 2 minutes or until spinach is just wilted. Stir spinach and prosciutto into hot cream.

❸ Transfer pasta to shallow bowl; sprinkle cheese over pasta. Pour cream mixture over cheese; toss gently but thoroughly. Season with additional salt, nutmeg and pepper. Divide pasta evenly among plates.

4 servings.

Preparation time: 15 minutes. Ready to serve: 20 minutes.

Per serving: 765 calories, 40 g total fat (24 g saturated fat), 140 mg cholesterol, 1180 mg sodium, 4.5 g fiber.

CAPANELLI WITH CAULIFLOWER AND DRIED TOMATOES

Both cauliflower and dried tomatoes are intensely flavored, but they don't fight with each other; rather, each accents the other in this ideal winter dish.

1	tablespoon kosher (coarse) salt plus more to taste
2	cups cauliflower florets, cut into 1½-inch pieces
2	tablespoons butter, softened
3	tablespoons sun-dried tomato tapenade
8 to 10	oz. capanelli (flower-shaped pasta) or other medium pasta shape
1	cup shredded Italian fontina cheese (4 oz.)
3	tablespoons minced kalamata olives
	Freshly ground pepper to taste

❶ Fill large pot two-thirds full of water; add 1 tablespoon salt. Bring to a boil over high heat. Blanch cauliflower in boiling water 2 minutes. Use strainer to transfer cauliflower to shallow bowl. Add butter and tapenade; toss with cauliflower. Cover bowl to keep warm.

❷ Cook capanelli in same pot according to package directions. Drain pasta thoroughly. Do not rinse. Add cooked pasta to bowl with cauliflower; toss gently but thoroughly. Add cheese and olives. Season with salt and pepper. Divide pasta evenly among plates.

4 servings.

Preparation time: 10 minutes.

Ready to serve: 25 minutes.

Per serving: 575 calories, 27 g total fat (13.5 g saturated fat), 60 mg cholesterol, 680 mg sodium, 4.5 g fiber.

SALMON WITH LEMON ROSAMARINA

You can prepare fresh tuna, swordfish and shark in this same way. And you can use any one of the seasoned Compound Butters *(pages 70-71) if you like. Bottom line? Experiment and have fun! Here is the basic idea.*

1   recipe *Rosamarina with Lemon Butter Seasoning* (page 71)
2   tablespoons butter
1   (1½-lb.) salmon fillet, cut into 1-inch pieces, skin and bones removed
1   tablespoon minced lemon peel
3/4 teaspoon minced fresh rosemary needles
    Kosher (coarse) salt to taste
    Freshly ground pepper to taste
4   small rosemary sprigs
1   lemon, cut in wedges

❶ Prepare Rosamarina with Lemon Butter Seasoning. Set aside.

❷ Melt butter in large skillet over high heat. Fry salmon, tossing frequently, 3 to 4 minutes or until salmon flakes easily with fork. Add lemon peel and rosemary needles. Season with salt and pepper; toss 2 or 3 times. Remove from heat.

❸ Divide rosamarina evenly among 4 plates; top each portion with salmon. Garnish with rosemary sprigs and lemon wedges.

4 servings.

Preparation time: 10 minutes. Ready to serve: 20 minutes.

Per serving: 530 calories, 22 g total fat (9 g saturated fat), 110 mg cholesterol, 470 mg sodium, 2.5 g fiber.

FETTUCCINE ALFREDO WITH ASIAGO AND FRESH PEAS

One of the great classic pastas, fettuccine Alfredo is deceptively simple and requires excellent ingredients. In this version, Asiago adds a tangy element, and fresh peas contribute a sweet and colorful note. If you do not have fresh peas, omit them rather than use frozen peas in their place.

1	tablespoon kosher (coarse) salt plus more to taste
1	recipe *One-Egg Pasta* (page 11), cut into fettuccine
3/4	cup fresh peas
2	tablespoons butter
1	shallot, minced
1	cup whipping cream
3/4	cup grated imported aged Asiago cheese (3 oz.)
	Freshly ground pepper to taste

❶ Fill large pot two-thirds full of water; add 1 tablespoon salt. Bring to a boil over high heat. Cook fettucine in boiling water 1½ to 2 minutes or until tender; drain. Do not rinse. Blanch peas for 3 minutes; refresh in ice water and drain. Set aside.

❷ Meanwhile, melt butter in medium skillet over medium heat. When foamy, add shallot; sauté about 5 minutes or until soft. Add cream; simmer until reduced by one-third. Remove from heat; stir in cheese and peas. Season with salt and pepper.

❸ Place cooked pasta in medium bowl; pour sauce over pasta. Toss gently but thoroughly. Divide pasta evenly among plates.

4 servings.

Preparation time: 45 minutes.

Ready to serve: 20 minutes.

Per serving: 640 calories, 43 g total fat (25 g saturated fat), 200 mg cholesterol, 1145 mg sodium, 3.5 g fiber.

CHERRY TOMATOES, PARSLEY, GARLIC, OLIVE OIL AND GNOCCHI

Because the tender little potato dumplings called gnocchi have become so popular in recent years, the name of this pasta might be confusing. Gnocchi is also a smallish pasta shape, similar to a shell but a little more open, so that sliced cherry tomatoes often wiggle inside them. If you don't have gnocchi, any medium-small pasta shape will do. This recipe is also pictured on pages 76 and 77.

1	tablespoon kosher (coarse) salt plus more to taste
1	lb. dried gnocchi (dumpling-shaped pasta)
3	cups ripe cherry tomatoes, halved or quartered
1	small red onion, diced
6	garlic cloves, minced
1/2	cup minced fresh Italian parsley
2	cups brocconcini cheese, quartered or 2 cups shredded fresh mozzarella (8 oz.)
	Freshly ground pepper to taste
1/4	cup extra-virgin olive oil

❶ Fill large pot two-thirds full of water; add 1 tablespoon salt. Bring to a boil over high heat. Cook gnocchi according to package directions; drain. Do not rinse.

❷ Combine cherry tomatoes, onion, garlic, parsley and cheese in large bowl; toss together gently. Season with salt and pepper; add olive oil. Add pasta to bowl and toss gently but thoroughly. Divide pasta evenly among bowls.

4 servings.
Preparation time: 15 minutes.
Ready to serve: 25 minutes.

Per serving: 755 calories, 36 g total fat (8 g saturated fat), 115 mg cholesterol, 870 mg sodium, 5 g fiber.

LINGUINE WITH HONEYED TOMATO SAUCE AND SHRIMP

There are many uncooked tomato sauces; they retain their fresh summery flavors and are warmed by the hot pasta when it is mixed in. If you've never paired fresh tomatoes with honey, this recipe might seem unusual at first glance, but it is actually quite delicious, especially with the sweet shrimp.

1	tablespoon plus 1 teaspoon kosher (coarse) salt
12	oz. dried linguine
5	large ripe tomatoes, peeled, seeded, minced
3	teaspoons minced garlic
1/2	cup lightly packed fresh basil leaves, cut into thin strips
1/4	cup extra-virgin olive oil
2	teaspoons freshly ground pepper
1	shallot, minced
3	tablespoons balsamic vinegar
3	tablespoons white wine or sherry vinegar
1/4	cup honey
1	lb. medium turtle-safe shrimp, peeled, deveined

❶ Fill large pot two-thirds full of water; add 1 tablespoon salt. Bring to a boil over high heat. Cook linguine according to package directions.

❷ Meanwhile, in large bowl, stir together tomatoes, 2 teaspoons of the minced garlic, basil and 2 tablespoons of the olive oil. Add remaining 1 teaspoon salt and 2 teaspoons pepper; set aside.

❸ Heat remaining 2 tablespoons olive oil in medium skillet; add shallot and remaining 1 teaspoon garlic. Sauté 2 minutes; stir in vinegars and honey. Add shrimp; cook about 2 minutes, turning once, until just pink. Remove skillet from heat; transfer shrimp to small plate and keep warm. Return skillet to medium heat. Add 3 tablespoons water; swirl. Stir juices into tomato sauce. In another large pot, bring tomato sauce to a boil over medium-high heat; boil 3 minutes to reduce sauce.

❹ Drain pasta thoroughly; do not rinse. Immediately toss sauce with cooked pasta. Divide pasta evenly among plates; top each portion with shrimp.

4 servings.

Preparation time: 35 minutes. Ready to serve: 55 minutes.

Per serving: 1140 calories, 70 g total fat (9 g saturated fat), 105 mg cholesterol, 880 mg sodium, 7 g fiber.

SIMPLE PASTAS
WHEN YOU HAVE A BIT MORE TIME

These recipes require a little more preparation time but they are not too demanding. There is no filling or wrapping necessary, for example. They do require ingredients you might not have on hand, so be sure to plan ahead by reading through the entire recipe before going to the market.

Little Ropes with Rib-Eye Steak, Grilled Onions and Gorgonzola Butter, page 116

LINGUINE WITH SWEET PEPPERS AND SHRIMP

This colorful and delicious dish takes advantage of the beautiful peppers available in the fall. Use any mix of colors that you can find, but do not substitute hot peppers for sweet ones. If you cannot find haricots verts — pencil-thin green beans — simply omit them.

1 lb. rock shrimp or small prawns, peeled, deveined

1 teaspoon chipotle powder

1 tablespoon kosher (coarse) salt plus more to taste

1 lb. dried linguine

Ginger Butter (recipe follows) or 1/3 cup extra-virgin olive oil

1 shallot, minced

2 red bell peppers, roasted, peeled, seeded, cut into matchstick-size strips

2 orange bell peppers, roasted, peeled, seeded, cut into matchstick-size strips

1 green bell pepper, roasted, peeled, seeded, cut into matchstick-size strips

1 lime, cut in half

Freshly ground pepper to taste

4 oz. haricots verts, blanched, refreshed in cold water

3/4 cup fresh bread crumbs, toasted

1 lime, cut in wedges

❶ In small bowl, toss together shrimp and chipotle powder; cover and refrigerate.

❷ Fill large pot two-thirds full of water; add 1 tablespoon salt. Bring to a boil over high heat. Cook linguine according to package directions; drain. Place in large serving bowl. Toss with one-half of Ginger Butter.

❸ Meanwhile, place remaining one-half Ginger Butter in medium skillet over medium heat. Add shallots and peppers; sauté 2 minutes or until soft and fragrant. Add shrimp; cook 3 to 4 minutes or until shrimp are pink.

④ Squeeze juice of 1 lime over shrimp and peppers. Season with salt and pepper; toss with pasta. Return skillet to medium-low heat; add haricots verts. Cook 3 minutes. Sprinkle bread crumbs over pasta; arrange haricots verts around outer edge. Garnish with lime wedges.

6 servings.
Preparation time: 1 hour, 15 minutes. Ready to serve: 1 hour, 45 minutes.

Per serving: 800 calories, 20 g total fat (10 g saturated fat), 200 mg cholesterol, 1310 mg sodium, 9 g fiber.

GINGER BUTTER

   1/3   cup unsalted butter, softened
     2   teaspoons grated fresh ginger
     2   teaspoons grated lime peel
     1   teaspoon minced garlic
   1/2   teaspoon kosher (coarse) salt
   1/2   teaspoon sugar
   1/2   teaspoon freshly ground
         pepper

❶ In small bowl, combine butter, ginger, lime, garlic, salt, sugar and pepper; mix with fork until smooth. Store in refrigerator, covered, 3 to 4 days or in freezer up to 1 month.

7 tablespoons.

Per serving (1 tablespoon): 80 calories, 9 g total fat (5 g saturated fat), 25 mg cholesterol, 110 mg sodium, 0 g fiber.

Ginger Butter *lends a spicy and refreshing twist to* Linguine with Sweet Peppers and Shrimp.

RIGATONI WITH BRAISED FENNEL, LEMON AND FRESH RICOTTA

Raw fennel is refreshing and crunchy, with a slight taste of licorice. When braised it becomes rich and almost sweet, and is best accented with a little lemon.

2	tablespoons olive oil
2	fennel bulbs, trimmed, cut into 1-inch-wide wedges
1	tablespoon kosher (coarse) salt plus more to taste
	Freshly ground pepper to taste
1/2	cup dry white wine
1/4	cup fresh lemon juice
1	lb. rigatoni (tube-shaped pasta)
1	cup fresh ricotta cheese (4 oz.)
2	teaspoons grated lemon peel
8	basil leaves, cut into thin crosswise strips

❶ Heat olive oil in medium skillet over medium heat until hot; add fennel and sauté, turning frequently, until cut edges begin to turn golden brown. Sprinkle with salt and pepper. Add wine and 2 tablespoons of the lemon juice. Reduce heat to low; cover and cook about 20 minutes or until fennel is very tender when pierced with fork. Remove saucepan from heat.

❷ Fill large pot two-thirds full of water; add 1 tablespoon salt. Bring to a boil over high heat. Cook rigatoni according to package directions; drain. Do not rinse. Transfer cooked pasta to shallow bowl.

❸ Add ricotta, braised fennel (with cooking juices), remaining 2 tablespoons lemon juice and lemon peel; toss gently until cheese is melted. Add basil leaves; season with salt and pepper. Toss again.

4 servings.
Preparation time: 10 minutes. Ready to serve: 35 minutes.

Per serving: 690 calories, 21 g total fat (5 g saturated fat), 20 mg cholesterol, 875 mg sodium, 7 g fiber.

FETTUCCINE WITH MUSHROOMS AND MARSALA

If you don't have specialty mushrooms, here's a little trick: Add 2 or 3 teaspoons of concentrated dried tomato paste; it will add a depth of flavor that doesn't exactly mimic that of more flavorful mushrooms, but comes close.

1	lb. wild mushrooms such as porcinis or chantrelles, or specialty mushrooms such as oyster, clamshell or portobello*
3	tablespoons butter
1	shallot, minced
1	tablespoon kosher (coarse) salt plus more to taste
	Freshly ground pepper to taste
1/3	cup Marsala wine
1	cup half-and-half
1	lb. dried fettuccine
1/2	cup whipping cream
2	tablespoons fresh-snipped chives or minced fresh Italian parsley
18	whole chives and chive flowers, individual blossoms separated

❶ Clean mushrooms with mushroom brush or damp cloth. Slice or break mushrooms into bite-size pieces. Melt butter in large skillet over medium heat. Sauté shallot 3 minutes or until soft and fragrant. Add mushrooms and sauté 5 minutes, stirring occasionally, until wilted. Season with salt and pepper; add wine; toss and simmer until reduced by half. Add half-and-half; cover and simmer until mushrooms are very tender.

❷ Meanwhile, fill large pot two-thirds full of water; add 1 tablespoon salt. Bring to a boil over high heat. Cook fettuccine according to package directions; drain. Do not rinse.

❸ Add whipping cream to mushroom mixture; cook an additional 5 to 6 minutes or until sauce thickens slightly. Stir in chives. Pour sauce over pasta and toss gently until evenly coated. Divide pasta evenly among plates; garnish with chives and chive flowers.

A nice Valpolicella, a dry red wine from Northern Italy, makes a great complement to the rustic taste of wild mushrooms in this dish.

4 servings.

Preparation time: 15 minutes. Ready to serve: 35 minutes.

Per serving: 680 calories, 30 g total fat (16.5 g saturated fat), 175 mg cholesterol, 880 mg sodium, 5 g fiber.

TIP *Do not use standard white mushrooms or shiitakes in this recipe. If your mushrooms lack flavor, you can use 1-ounce dried porcinis. Cover the dried mushrooms with hot water to soften them; mince the softened mushrooms and add them to the cooked shallots. Strain the cooking liquid through a fine strainer or cheesecloth, and add it to the sauce with the half-and-half.

POTATO-PASTA CASSEROLE WITH MUSHROOMS AND FONTINA

Pairing pasta with potatoes is not as unusual as you may think; their textures work well together, as do their slightly earthy flavors, which are heightened in this recipe by the addition of mushrooms.

 1 tablespoon kosher (coarse) salt plus more to taste
12 oz. ditalini (short macaroni tubes)
 3 tablespoons olive oil
 1 yellow onion, minced
 4 garlic cloves, minced
 3 oz. pancetta, minced
 8 oz. portobello mushrooms, trimmed, diced
    Freshly ground pepper to taste
 2 cups *Chicken Stock* (page 22)
 1 lb. new red potatoes, scrubbed, diced 1/2-inch thick
1/4 cup minced fresh Italian parsley
 2 eggs, beaten
 1 cup whipping cream or half-and-half
 1 cup shredded Italian fontina cheese (4 oz.)

❶ Fill large pot two-thirds full of water; add 1 tablespoon salt. Bring to a boil over high heat. Cook ditalini according to package directions. Rinse and drain pasta thoroughly in cool water.

❷ Heat oven to 350°F. Spray large casserole with nonstick cooking spray. Heat olive oil in large skillet over medium heat until hot; sauté onion about 5 minutes or until soft and fragrant. Add garlic and pancetta; sauté, stirring frequently, 5 to 6 minutes or until pancetta is translucent. Add mushrooms; stir and sauté 2 minutes. Season with salt and pepper. Add 1 cup of the Chicken Stock; simmer until mushrooms are soft and stock is nearly evaporated. Add potatoes; stir and sauté 3 minutes. Remove mixture from heat and fold in parsley and cooked pasta.

❸ In small bowl, mix together remaining chicken stock, eggs and cream; pour mixture over pasta and vegetables. Fold in fontina; pour mixture into casserole. Cover and bake 15 minutes. Uncover and bake an additional 10 minutes or until top begins to turn golden brown. Remove from oven; let stand 5 minutes before serving.

8 servings.
Preparation time: 15 minutes. Ready to serve: 1 hour, 10 minutes.

Per serving: 700 calories, 40 g total fat (18 g saturated fat), 145 mg cholesterol, 755 mg sodium, 5 g fiber.

PASTA AL CEPPO WITH PANCETTA, SHALLOTS, ARTICHOKES, OLIVES AND CHICKEN

The cream here is what ties all the other ingredients together and serves as a medium to their juices and flavors, bringing them to the pasta.

1	teaspoon plus 2 tablespoons olive oil
2	artichokes, trimmed
2	teaspoons plus 1 tablespoon kosher (coarse) salt plus more to taste
1	(1-lb.) pkg. pasta al ceppo or other medium-length pasta
2	shallots, thinly sliced
2	garlic cloves, minced
3	oz. pancetta, minced
	Freshly ground pepper to taste
1/2	cup cracked green olives, pitted, sliced
8	oz. cooked chicken meat, cut into matchstick-size strips
3	tablespoons minced fresh Italian parsley
3/4	cup whipping cream
2	cups shredded fresh mozzarella (8 oz.)

❶ In medium saucepan, drizzle 1 teaspoon of the olive oil into center of each artichoke; add water to cover. Add 2 teaspoons salt to water; bring to a boil over medium-high heat. Reduce heat to medium-low; simmer 20 to 40 minutes or until artichokes are tender. Drain; rinse in cool water. Turn upside down on clean kitchen towel to drain thoroughly. When artichokes are cool, remove leaves. Use paring knife to cut out fuzzy choke in center of heart. Cut away any dark green parts on bottom of hearts. Reserve leaves for another use. Cut hearts into crosswise slices about 1/6-inch thick. Set aside.

❷ Fill large pot two-thirds full of water; add 1 tablespoon salt. Bring to a boil over high heat. Cook pasta al ceppo according to package directions; drain. Do not rinse.

❸ Heat remaining 2 tablespoons olive oil in medium skillet over medium heat; add shallots. Sauté 7 to 8 minutes or until soft and fragrant. Add garlic; sauté an additional 2 minutes. Add pancetta; sauté 5 minutes or

An authentic foccaccia is all you need to turn this hearty pasta into a memorable meal.

until translucent. Season with salt and pepper, olives, chicken, parsley and cream; simmer 5 minutes. Remove from heat. Transfer hot pasta into warmed serving bowl; add mozzarella and toss thoroughly. Pour sauce over pasta; toss again. Divide pasta evenly among plates.

4 to 6 servings.

Preparation time: 1 hour, 10 minutes. Ready to serve: 1 hour, 15 minutes.

Per serving: 1090 calories, 56 g total fat (22 g saturated fat), 135 mg cholesterol, 1735 mg sodium, 8 g fiber.

BAKED TOMATOES STUFFED WITH ORZO, HERBS AND ZUCCHINI

For the best-tasting tomatoes, buy them only when they are in season, usually from July through October or November. These tomatoes make an excellent accompaniment to roasted chicken.

1 tablespoon kosher (coarse) salt plus more to taste

3/4 cup dry orzo (rice-shaped pasta) (3 oz.)

4 medium tomatoes

   Freshly ground pepper to taste

1 tablespoon extra-virgin olive oil

1 teaspoon minced garlic

2 small zucchini, diced

1 teaspoon minced fresh Italian parsley

1 teaspoon minced fresh oregano

1 teaspoon minced fresh thyme

4 teaspoons freshly grated Parmigiano-Reggiano cheese (3/4 oz.)

❶ Heat oven to 350°F. Fill large pot two-thirds full of water; add 1 tablespoon salt. Bring to a boil over high heat. Cook orzo according to package directions; drain. Rinse and drain pasta thoroughly under cool water.

❷ Meanwhile, cut off stem end of each tomato into 1/4-inch-thick slices. Discard ends; use spoon to scoop out and discard seeds and pulp from tomato, leaving shell. Season inside with salt and pepper.

❸ Heat olive oil in small saucepan over medium-low heat until hot. Add garlic; sauté 1 minute. Add zucchini; sauté 3 to 4 minutes. Add herbs; season with salt and pepper. Remove from heat.

❹ Toss zucchini mixture with cooked pasta; fill each tomato with orzo-zucchini mixture. Sprinkle 1 teaspoon cheese over each tomato; bake 20 minutes or until tomatoes soften and are sizzling hot.

4 servings.

Preparation time: 15 minutes. Ready to serve: 35 minutes.

Per serving: 200 calories, 11 g total fat (2 g saturated fat), 1 mg cholesterol, 410 mg sodium, 2 g fiber.

PASTA PRIMAVERA

The traditional version of this classic pasta, the name of which means spring pasta, calls for vegetables that actually are ready in the summer. But you can easily vary this recipe and make a wonderful dish with spring vegetables.

2	teaspoons olive oil
1/2	lb. asparagus, cut into 2-inch pieces
3 to 4	spring onions, trimmed, cut into medium matchstick-size strips
1	tablespoon kosher (coarse) salt plus more to taste
	Freshly ground pepper to taste
3	tablespoons unsalted butter
4	spring garlic cloves, thinly sliced
1	lb. English peas (unshelled weight), shelled, blanched
3/4	cup shelled fresh fava beans, blanched, peeled
1	cup whipping cream
1	recipe *Two-Egg Pasta* (page 12), cut into fettuccine
3	oz. prosciutto, sliced 1/8-inch thick, cut into 1/4-inch crosswise strips
2	tablespoons fresh snipped chives
1	tablespoon chive flowers (individual flowers separated from main blossom)

❶ Heat oven to 450°F. In medium bowl, drizzle olive oil over asparagus and onions, tossing to coat vegetables thoroughly. Season with salt and pepper; spread on baking sheet in single layer. Bake 16 minutes or until vegetables are just tender.

❷ Melt butter in medium skillet over medium heat; add garlic and sauté 1 minute. Add peas, favas, asparagus and onions; toss together. Add cream; simmer 5 minutes. Season with salt and pepper; remove from heat.

❸ Meanwhile, fill large pot two-thirds full of water; add 1 tablespoon salt. Bring to a boil over high heat. Cook pasta in boiling water 1 1/2 minutes or until just tender. Drain; transfer cooked pasta to shallow bowl.

4 Pour vegetable mixture over pasta; toss together gently. Add prosciutto and snipped chives; toss again. Divide pasta evenly among plates; sprinkle chive flowers over each portion.

6 servings.

Preparation time: 1 hour. Ready to serve: 1 hour, 10 minutes.

Per serving: 615 calories, 34 g total fat (18.5 g saturated fat), 155 mg cholesterol, 895 mg sodium, 13 g fiber.

FETTUCCINE WITH SHIITAKES, PEAS AND PROSCIUTTO

Fettuccine is designed to be served with a creamy sauce, which clings to the wide surface of the noodles.

1 tablespoon kosher (coarse) salt plus more to taste
8 oz. dried fettuccine
2 tablespoons olive oil
2 oz. prosciutto, diced
8 oz. shiitake mushrooms, stems removed, thinly sliced
3/4 cup *Chicken Stock* (page 22), dry white wine or water
   Freshly ground pepper to taste
1/2 cup half-and-half
1 cup (about 4 oz.) frozen petite peas, thawed
3 tablespoons minced fresh Italian parsley

❶ Fill large pot two-thirds full of water; add 1 tablespoon salt. Bring to a boil over high heat. Cook fettuccine according to package directions; drain. Do not rinse.

❷ Meanwhile, heat olive oil in large skillet over medium heat until hot. Add prosciutto; sauté 2 minutes. Add mushrooms and Chicken Stock; season with salt and pepper. Cover and simmer 5 to 6 minutes or until mushrooms are soft. Uncover and simmer until liquid is nearly evaporated.

❸ Add half-and-half and peas; stir and heat through. Season generously with pepper; add drained fettuccine. Toss quickly; remove from heat. Divide pasta evenly among warmed dinner plates. Top each portion with Italian parsley.

3 to 4 servings.

Preparation time: 15 minutes. Ready to serve: 20 minutes.

Per serving: 490 calories, 19 g total fat (5.5 g saturated fat), 90 mg cholesterol, 1220 mg sodium, 5.5 g fiber.

FARFALLONE WITH MOZZARELLA FRESCA, GREEN OLIVES, PROSCIUTTO AND CELERY

You'll need to cut the prosciutto slice-by-slice; if you stack the strips on top of each other, they will stick together. The pasta is thick and flat, with a rougher surface than most other domestic commercial pastas. It is substantial and full of the good flavor and texture of hard winter wheat, from which it is made.

1	tablespoon kosher (coarse) salt plus more to taste
12	oz. farfallone
2	tablespoons olive oil
1/2	cup chopped red onion
5	ribs celery, trimmed, cut into 1/4-inch diagonal slices
	Freshly ground pepper to taste
2	cups fresh mozzarella, cut into 1/4x11/4-inch pieces (8 oz.)
1/4	lb. prosciutto, sliced 1/16-inch thick, cut into 2-inch-wide strips
4	oz. pitted Sicilian-style green olives, sliced lengthwise
1/3	cup extra-virgin olive oil

❶ Fill large pot two-thirds full of water; add 1 tablespoon salt. Bring to a boil over high heat. Cook farfallone according to package directions; drain. Do not rinse.

❷ Heat olive oil in medium skillet over medium heat until hot. Sauté onions about 5 minutes or until soft and fragrant. Add celery; sauté about 6 minutes or until tender. Season with salt and pepper; set aside. When pasta is nearly done, return celery mixture to heat and heat through.

❸ Transfer mozzarella, prosciutto and olives to shallow bowl; add cooked pasta and hot celery mixture. Toss thoroughly until cheese begins to melt. Drizzle with olive oil. Divide pasta evenly among plates.

4 servings.

Preparation time: 20 minutes. Ready to serve: 35 minutes.

Per serving: 685 calories, 40 g total fat (8 g saturated fat), 110 mg cholesterol, 1875 mg sodium, 4 g fiber.

INDIVIDUAL LASAGNE WITH PORTOBELLO, ACORN SQUASH AND MOZZARELLA FRESCA

Serve this rich lasagne with a lean soup and a crisp green salad.

- 1 acorn squash or other winter squash, peeled
- 1/2 cup *Clarified Butter* (page 18)
- 4 medium portobello mushrooms, washed, trimmed, stems removed
- 1 tablespoon kosher (coarse) salt plus more to taste
  Freshly ground pepper to taste
- 2 cups fresh mozzarella, cut into thin slices (8 oz.)
- 12 egg roll wrappers
- 2 tablespoons minced fresh Italian parsley
- 2 tablespoons olive oil
- 1 cup freshly grated Parmigiano-Reggiano cheese (4 oz.)

❶ Heat oven to 375°F. Cut squash in half lengthwise; cut each half into 1/4-inch-thick slices. (You'll need 12 half-moon slices for this recipe; reserve any leftover squash for another recipe.)

❷ Melt 1/4 cup of the butter in medium skillet. Brush both sides of each mushroom lightly with butter; season with salt and pepper. Bake in 13x9-inch pan about 20 minutes or until very tender when pierced with fork.

❸ Sauté sliced squash in butter until tender and just golden brown on both sides. Season with salt and pepper; transfer to plate and keep warm. Add remaining 1/4 cup butter to skillet; heat butter over medium-high heat until it turns golden brown. Remove from heat and keep warm.

❹ Fill medium pot two-thirds full with water; add 1 tablespoon salt. Bring to a boil over high heat.

❺ Brush 4 serving plates with a little olive oil. Cook 4 egg roll wrappers in boiling water 45 to 60 seconds or until tender. When first batch of wrappers is cooked, set one on each plate. Cook second batch of wrappers; set aside. Top first wrapper with 2 slices of squash; season with pepper and parsley. Top with slice of mozzarella. Place second batch of wrappers on top of each portion. Cook third batch of wrappers; while they cook, set mushroom on

top of each portion. Divide remaining mozzarella over mushrooms. Season with salt, pepper and 2 tablespoons Italian parsley. Set third wrapper on top and add half-moon of squash on top of wrapper. If butter has solidified, quickly melt and spoon some over each serving. Sprinkle with Parmigiano-Reggiano cheese.

4 servings.

Preparation time: 30 minutes. Ready to serve: 40 minutes.

Per serving: 720 calories, 40 g total fat (25 g saturated fat), 155 mg cholesterol, 950 mg sodium, 3.5 g fiber.

TRENNE WITH BROCCOLI RAAB, GARLIC AND SOPPRESSATTA

Soppressatta is a type of Italian salami, a highly flavorful cured meat. It is so far superior to the salami we are used to, that it is hard to describe. Soppressatta is the perfect foil to the bitterness of broccoli raab.

1 tablespoon kosher (coarse) salt plus more to taste

12 oz. trenne, penne or other medium pasta shape

2 tablespoons olive oil

1/4 lb. soppressatta, cut into matchstick-size strips

4 garlic cloves, pressed

1 lb. broccoli raab, large tough stems trimmed away
  Freshly ground pepper to taste

1/2 teaspoon crushed red pepper

1 cup *Chicken Stock* (page 22)

1/2 cup freshly grated Parmigiano-Reggiano cheese (2 oz.)

❶ Fill large pot two-thirds full of hot water; add 1 tablespoon salt. Bring to a boil over high heat. Cook trenne according to package directions; drain. Do not rinse. Transfer cooked pasta to shallow bowl.

❷ Meanwhile, heat olive oil in large skillet over medium heat until hot; add soppressatta and garlic. Sauté 2 minutes; add broccoli raab. Toss thoroughly. Season with salt and pepper, add crushed red pepper and Chicken Stock.

❸ Cover and simmer 3 to 4 minutes or until stock is nearly evaporated. Toss with pasta. Divide evenly among plates; grate cheese over each portion. Pass remaining cheese and grater.

4 servings.

Preparation time: 15 minutes. Ready to serve: 35 minutes.

Per serving: 600 calories, 23 g total fat (7.5 g saturated fat), 35 mg cholesterol, 1440 mg sodium, 6 g fiber.

ORECCHIETTE WITH CABBAGE, SAUSAGE AND WHITE BEANS

You'll want to make this pasta in the winter, when it's cold outside and you're longing for rich, warming foods. If you don't have orecchiette, you can use dried gnocchi instead.

3/4 lb. spicy Italian sausage, casing removed
1   yellow onion, diced
1   lb. green cabbage, cut into lengthwise strips
1   teaspoon fresh thyme leaves, minced
3/4 cup dry white wine
1   tablespoon kosher (coarse) salt plus more to taste
12 oz. orecchiette (disk-shaped pasta)
2   cups cooked cannellini beans
    Freshly ground pepper to taste
1/2 cup extra-virgin olive oil

❶ Cook sausage in medium sauté pan over medium heat, breaking up meat with fork, until meat is no longer pink in center; discard fat. Add onion; cook 10 minutes or until tender. Add cabbage, thyme and wine; reduce heat to low. Cover and simmer 20 to 25 minutes or until cabbage is tender.

❷ Fill large pot two-thirds full of hot water; add 1 tablespoon salt. Bring to a boil over high heat. Cook orecchiette according to package directions; drain, reserving 1/4 cup of the cooking water.

❸ Add beans to cabbage; toss gently and heat through. Season with salt and pepper.

❹ Transfer cooked pasta to shallow bowl. Add cabbage mixture; toss gently. If mixture seems dry, add reserved cooking water. Divide pasta evenly among plates; drizzle each portion with 1 to 2 teaspoons olive oil.

4 to 6 servings.
Preparation time: 15 minutes. Ready to serve: 40 minutes.

Per serving: 685 calories, 18 g total fat (5 g saturated fat), 35 mg cholesterol, 1040 mg sodium, 10 g fiber.

CLASSIC SUMMER PESTO

The popularity of pesto has eclipsed its seasonal nature — it is, essentially, a summer sauce, best made when basil is fresh in your garden or at the farmers' market. Pesto should never be cooked. Not only does it turn nearly black when exposed to high temperatures, its taste becomes cloying and almost bitter.

- 1 tablespoon kosher (coarse) salt plus more to taste
- 1 lb. dried linguine or fettuccine
- 6 garlic cloves, crushed
- 1/2 cup fresh Italian parsley leaves, coarsely chopped
- 4 cups fresh basil leaves, coarsely chopped
- 1/2 cup extra-virgin olive oil
- 4 tablespoons butter, softened
- 3/4 cup grated Parmigiano-Reggiano cheese (3 oz.)
- 1/2 cup grated pecorino cheese (2 oz.)
- 3/4 cup walnut pieces, lightly toasted, minced

❶ Fill large pot two-thirds full of water; add 1 tablespoon salt. Bring to a boil over high heat. Cook pasta according to package directions; drain, reserving 1/4 cup of the cooking water. Do not rinse pasta. Transfer to shallow bowl.

❷ Meanwhile, combine garlic and salt in food processor; grind until nearly reduced to paste. Add small handful of parsley and larger handful of basil; grind chopped leaves against side of ridged bowl, crushing gently. When fairly well ground, add more leaves. Continue to grind until all parsley and basil have been incorporated. Stir in olive oil and butter; use rubber spatula to fold in cheeses. Taste; season with salt. Fold in walnuts.

❸ Stir reserved 1/4 cup cooking water into pesto; spoon one-half of pesto over pasta. Toss gently but thoroughly until pasta is evenly coated with sauce. Divide pasta evenly among plates, passing remaining pesto.

4 servings.
Preparation time: 10 minutes. Ready to serve: 20 minutes.
Per serving: 1095 calories, 65 g total fat (20 g saturated fat), 60 mg cholesterol, 1490 mg sodium, 6 g fiber.

LITTLE ROPES WITH RIB-EYE STEAK, GRILLED ONIONS AND GORGONZOLA BUTTER

The Gorgonzola butter will keep, wrapped tightly and stored in the refrigerator, for one week. Toss leftover butter with steamed green beans or hot pasta.

1	tablespoon kosher (coarse) salt plus more to taste
8 to 10	oz. pasta al ceppo, gemelli or strozzapreti
1/2	cup unsalted butter, softened
3/4	cup Italian Gorgonzola cheese (3 oz.)
2	teaspoons minced fresh rosemary
2	teaspoons freshly ground pepper plus more to taste
1	red onion, peeled
2	teaspoons olive oil
2	beef rib-eye steaks, 1 1/2 inches thick
4	small rosemary sprigs

❶ Heat grill. Fill large pot two-thirds full of water; add 1 tablespoon salt. Bring to a boil over high heat. Cook al ceppo according to package directions; drain. Do not rinse.

❷ Meanwhile, in food processor, combine butter, Gorgonzola, rosemary and 2 teaspoons pepper; pulse about 15 seconds or until mixture comes together. Scrape sides with rubber spatula; pulse again. Transfer mixture to sheet of plastic wrap; wrap butter loosely and roll into log about 1 1/4 inches in diameter. Wrap tightly; place in freezer while preparing onion and steaks.

❸ Cut onion in half crosswise; rub with olive oil. Place on gas grill over medium-high heat or on charcoal grill 4 to 6 inches from medium-high coals. Grill onion, turning occasionally, 15 to 20 minutes or until tender; set aside.

❹ Season steaks on both sides with salt and pepper. Grill steaks 3 minutes; turn. Cook an additional 3 minutes; turn again, rotating direction to mark steaks. For rare steaks, cook about 2 minutes; turn and cook an additional 2 minutes. Remove from grill; cover with aluminum foil and let stand 5 minutes.

❺ Cut grilled onion into thin horizontal strips. Place cooked pasta and onion strips in medium bowl; cut several rounds of Gorgonzola butter and toss with pasta until butter is melted. Cut steaks into ¼-inch-thick diagonal strips; add to pasta. Season with salt and pepper; toss quickly. Divide pasta evenly among serving plates; garnish each portion with rosemary sprig.

4 servings.

Preparation time: 20 minutes. Ready to serve: 30 minutes.

Per serving: 1120 calories, 75 g total fat (35 g saturated fat), 240 mg cholesterol, 950 mg sodium, 3 g fiber.

PAPARDELLE WITH ZUCCHINI RIBBONS, PROSCIUTTO AND WARM TOMATO VINAIGRETTE

The best way to cut zucchini into thin strips is to use a mandoline, available in specialty cookware stores and catalogs. If you can't find yellow zucchini, use all green.

> Tomato Vinaigrette (recipe follows)
> 1 tablespoon kosher (coarse) salt plus more to taste
> 1 (8-oz.) pkg. papardelle pasta
> 2 green zucchini, cut into thin lengthwise strips
> 1 yellow zucchini, cut into thin crosswise strips
> 2 to 3 tablespoons olive oil
> Freshly ground pepper to taste
> 8 slices prosciutto, 1/8-inch thick, cut in half crosswise

❶ Prepare Tomato Vinaigrette; set aside.

❷ Fill large pot two-thirds full of water; add 1 tablespoon salt. Bring to a boil over high heat. Cook papardelle according to package directions; drain. Do not rinse. Transfer pasta to shallow bowl.

❸ Heat stove-top grill. Brush zucchini strips on both sides with olive oil; season with salt and pepper. Grill, turning twice, until cooked through and tender. Return Tomato Vinaigrette to heat; heat through.

❹ Toss grilled zucchini and prosciutto strips with pasta in shallow bowl. Divide pasta evenly among plates; spoon vinaigrette over each portion. Garnish with basil leaves, if desired.

3 to 4 servings.

Preparation time: 20 minutes. Ready to serve: 20 minutes.

Per serving: 825 calories, 45 g total fat (8 g saturated fat), 65 mg cholesterol, 2620 mg sodium, 6 g fiber.

TOMATO VINAIGRETTE

1 tablespoon olive oil

1 shallot, minced

2 garlic cloves, minced

2 tablespoons white wine or champagne vinegar

1/2 cup *Tomato Concassé* (page 19)

Kosher (coarse) salt to taste

Freshly ground pepper to taste

6 fresh basil leaves, cut into thin crosswise strips

1/3 cup extra-virgin olive oil

❶ Heat olive oil in small skillet over medium-low heat; sauté shallot about 5 minutes or until soft. Add garlic; sauté an additional 2 minutes. Stir in vinegar and Tomato Concassé; simmer 2 minutes.

❷ Season with salt, pepper, basil leaves and 1/3 cup extra-virgin olive oil. Heat through and remove from heat. Reheat sauce before serving.

4 servings.

Per serving: 200 calories, 20 g total fat (3 g saturated fat), 0 mg cholesterol, 340 mg sodium, .5 g fiber.

ACINI DI PEPE WITH PORTOBELLOS, FAVAS AND ASIAGO

There's something about the way this little round pasta, named for peppercorns, teases the palate. It is so delightful and compelling that you don't want to quit eating it. If you don't have fresh favas, use fresh spring peas or omit them entirely.

1	tablespoon kosher (coarse) salt plus more to taste
8	oz. acini di pepe (peppercorn-shaped pasta)
2	tablespoons olive oil
2	oz. pancetta, diced
1	red onion, diced
2	portobello mushrooms, trimmed, diced
3/4	cup dry white wine
	Freshly ground pepper to taste
3/4	cup shelled fava beans (from 1 lb. of beans in pods), blanched, peeled
1	cup grated aged Italian Asiago cheese (4 oz.)

❶ Fill large pot two-thirds full of water; add 1 tablespoon salt. Bring to a boil over high heat. Cook acini de pepe according to package directions; drain. Rinse and drain thoroughly in cool water. Transfer cooked pasta to medium bowl. Drizzle with 1 tablespoon of the olive oil; toss to coat thoroughly.

❷ Heat oven to 350°F. Heat remaining 1 tablespoon olive oil in medium skillet over medium heat until hot. Cook pancetta about 5 minutes or until translucent. Add onion; sauté 5 minutes. Add mushrooms; sauté until soft and begin to lose moisture, stirring frequently.

❸ Add wine; toss mixture. Simmer until wine is nearly evaporated, about 10 minutes. Season with salt and pepper. Add pancetta mixture and favas to pasta bowl; toss gently but thoroughly. Stir in 1/2 cup of the cheese; pour mixture into shallow baking dish. Sprinkle remaining 1/2 cup cheese over pasta; bake about 15 minutes or until cheese is melted and just turning golden brown. Remove from oven; let stand 5 minutes before serving.

4 servings.

Preparation time: 30 minutes. Ready to serve: 1 hour.

Per serving: 585 calories, 29 g total fat (11 g saturated fat), 35 mg cholesterol, 1125 mg sodium, 5 g fiber.

FUSILLI COL BUCO WITH ONIONS, BACON, LENTILS AND SAGE

Fusilli col buco resembles long, curly strands of hair, perfect for trapping lentils and bits of bacon. If you prepare the lentils or even the entire sauce the day before serving this pasta, your final preparation time won't be long at all.

    Cooked Lentils (recipe follows on page 124)
3   tablespoons *Clarified Butter* (page 18)
2   red onions, very thinly sliced
1   tablespoon kosher (coarse) salt plus more to taste
1   cup full-bodied red wine
2   teaspoons sugar
6   bacon slices, diced*
    Freshly ground pepper to taste
12 oz. fusilli col buco
6   medium sage leaves, minced
6   sage sprigs

❶ Prepare Cooked Lentils; set aside.

❷ Melt butter in wide saucepan over medium heat; toss onions in butter. Season with salt; cook, stirring occasionally, 7 or 8 minutes or until wilted. Add wine; reduce heat to low. Cover and simmer 30 minutes. Uncover and continue to cook onions, stirring occasionally to avoid burning, 1 1/4 hours or until they are nearly melted, very sweet, and all liquid is evaporated. (If onions are not sweet, stir in sugar and continue to cook until rich and flavorful.) Remove from heat.

❸ Cook bacon in small skillet over medium heat until just crispy. Using slotted spoon, transfer bacon to paper towels and discard bacon fat. (If using mushroom instead of bacon, heat olive oil; add mushroom. Season with salt and pepper; sauté about 12 minutes or until very soft.)

❹ Fill large pot two-thirds full of water; add 1 tablespoon salt. Bring to a boil over high heat. Cook fusilli col buco according to package directions; drain. Do not rinse. Transfer pasta to shallow bowl.

122

❺ Over low heat, stir lentils into caramelized onions; add sage.

❻ Top pasta with hot lentil mixture; toss thoroughly. Add bacon or mushrooms; toss gently. Divide pasta evenly among plates. Garnish each portion with sage sprigs.

TIP *Substitute with 1 medium portobello mushroom, trimmed, diced plus 1 tablespoon olive oil.

6 servings.

Preparation time: 30 minutes. Ready to serve: 4 hours.

Per serving: 430 calories, 11 g total fat (5 g saturated fat), 25 mg cholesterol, 710 mg sodium, 8 g fiber.

Continued on page 124

Continued from page 123

COOKED LENTILS

For use in Fusilli col Buco with Onions, Bacon, Lentils and Sage.

3/4 cup brown or green lentils, rinsed

1 yellow onion, cut in half

4 garlic cloves

1 carrot, cut into chunks

1 rib celery, cut into chunks

1 leek, cleaned, trimmed

3 fresh Italian parsley sprigs

1 bay leaf

2 teaspoons kosher (coarse) salt

❶ In medium pot, combine lentils, onion, garlic, carrot, celery, leek, parsley sprigs and bay leaf. Add water to cover plus 1 inch. Add salt; bring to a boil over high heat. Reduce heat to medium-low; use wide spoon to skim off foam. Simmer about 30 minutes or until lentils are tender. Remove from heat; strain lentils and reserve cooking liquid.

❷ Place lentil mixture in medium bowl. Remove and discard onion, garlic, carrot, celery, leek, parsley and bay leaf. Stir 1/2 cup of cooking liquid back into lentils. Reserve remaining liquid for another use.

Preparation time: 20 minutes.
Ready to serve: 30 minutes.

Per serving: 165 calories, .5 g total fat (0 g saturated fat), 0 mg cholesterol, 430 mg sodium, 11 g fiber.

ORECCHIETTE WITH BROCCOLI AND TOASTED GARLIC

As garlic toasts, it develops a slightly sweet and nutty taste. Be sure to cook it slowly until golden brown; do not let it burn.

1	tablespoon kosher (coarse) salt plus more to taste
1	lb. dried orecchiette
1	lb. broccoli florets
6	garlic cloves, thinly sliced
1/4	cup extra-virgin olive oil
4	anchovy fillets, drained, minced
1	garlic clove, minced
1/2	teaspoon crushed red pepper
	Freshly ground pepper to taste

❶ Fill large pot two-thirds full with water; add 1 tablespoon salt. Bring to a boil over high heat. Cook orecchiette according to package directions until al dente; drain. Transfer pasta to large shallow bowl.

❷ Meanwhile, steam broccoli over boiling water until just tender, about 4 minutes. In heavy skillet, toast garlic over medium-low heat, tossing frequently, until lightly browned and just crisp, about 4 minutes. Set aside.

❸ In small bowl, combine oil, anchovy fillets and minced garlic. Add broccoli to pasta; toss together lightly. Add garlic mixture. Season with crushed red pepper, salt and pepper; toss again. Divide pasta evenly among plates; top each portion with toasted garlic. Serve immediately.

4 servings.

Preparation time: 15 minutes.
Ready to serve: 25 minutes.

Per serving: 640 calories, 20 g total fat (3 g saturated fat),
2 mg cholesterol, 830 mg sodium, 7.5 g fiber.

ZUCCHINI AND PESTO LASAGNE

Enjoy this full-flavored lasagne.

4	zucchini, trimmed, cut into $1/8$-inch-thick lengthwise slices
$2^1/2$	tablespoons olive oil
1	tablespoon kosher (coarse) salt plus more to taste
2	cups whipping cream
$1^1/2$	cups fresh pesto (page 115)
12	egg roll wrappers
6	cups fresh ricotta (24 oz.)
$1/2$	cup freshly grated Parmigiano-Reggiano cheese (2 oz.)
4	small fresh basil sprigs

❶ Heat grill or set a heavy-ridged pan over medium heat. Brush zucchini slices on both sides lightly with olive oil; season with salt. Place zucchini strips on gas grill over medium heat or on charcoal grill 4 to 6 inches from medium coals. Cook 2 to 3 minutes per side or until they just begin to turn golden brown and tender. Set aside and keep warm.

❷ Heat cream to a boil in medium saucepan over medium heat. Stir in pesto; remove from heat. Keep warm. Fill medium pot two-thirds full of water; add 1 tablespoon salt. Bring to a boil over high heat.

❸ Brush 4 serving plates with a little olive oil. Cook 4 egg roll wrappers in boiling water 45 to 60 seconds or until tender. When first batch of wrappers is cooked, set one on each plate. Top each wrapper with one quarter of the ricotta; spoon about 3 tablespoons hot pesto cream sauce over ricotta. Cook second batch of wrappers; place 1 wrapper on top of each portion. Drape zucchini over second wrappers, reserving 4 slices. Spoon pesto cream sauce over top. Cook third batch of wrappers; set one on top of each serving. Drape zucchini slice over each serving; spoon sauce on top. Sprinkle with cheese; garnish with basil sprig.

4 servings.
Preparation time: 20 minutes. Ready to serve: 30 minutes.
Per serving: 1560 calories, 125 g total fat (50 g saturated fat), 250 mg cholesterol, 3210 mg sodium, 6 g fiber.

SCALLOPS WITH LEMON SORREL SAUCE AND SQUID-INK GEMELLI

Sorrel is a green similar in appearance to spinach, though the leaves grow much bigger. It has a tangy flavor that resembles lemon.

3/4 cup fresh bread crumbs, lightly toasted

1 tablespoon kosher (coarse) salt plus more to taste

1 lb. bay scallops, rinsed, dried on clean kitchen towel

10 oz. squid-ink gemelli, tagliarini or strozzapreti

1 cup whipping cream

4 cups stemmed and shredded fresh sorrel

3 tablespoons *Clarified Butter* (page 18)

1 tablespoon grated lemon peel

8 thin lemon slices

❶ In small bowl, season bread crumbs with salt. Add scallops; toss thoroughly. Transfer scallops to parchment paper. Set aside.

❷ Fill large pot two-thirds full of water; add 1 tablespoon salt. Bring to a boil over high heat. Cook gemelli according to package directions; drain. Do not rinse. Transfer cooked pasta to shallow bowl.

❸ Meanwhile, heat cream in small saucepan over medium heat until hot. Combine sorrel and hot cream in blender; pulse until mixture is evenly blended and uniformly green. Strain mixture into clean saucepan; season with salt and pepper. Set aside.

❹ Melt Clarified Butter in large skillet over medium-high heat; add scallops. Sauté, tossing frequently, 5 minutes or until scallops are evenly browned and opaque. Cooked scallops will be somewhat firm when pressed; do not over-cook. Warm sorrel sauce over medium heat; add lemon peel and heat through, but do not boil. Pour sauce over pasta; toss lightly. Divide pasta evenly among plates; top each portion with scallops. Garnish with lemon slices.

4 servings.

Preparation time: 15 minutes. Ready to serve: 20 minutes.

Per serving: 720 calories, 34 g total fat (20 g saturated fat), 135 mg cholesterol, 1375 mg sodium, 4 g fiber.

PASTA FOR WEEKENDS

AND SPECIAL OCCASIONS

We sometimes make elaborate meals on the weekends or for special occasions – not because we have to, but because devoting several hours to such a project is both fun and satisfying. Some of these pastas can become projects for the entire family. The ideas here are for special occasions, those times when we want to indulge in the rich foods and flavors we avoid most of the time.

Pasta Frittata, page 144

POTATO RAVIOLI WITH EGGS AND TRUFFLES

Here is a delicate dish that requires not so much time as a bit of tenderness. You must be careful to not break the egg yolks and to cook them enough — but not too much. The result is dazzling.

2 russet potatoes (about 1 lb.), scrubbed

1$^1/_2$ cups peeled diced celery root (about 1 lb.)

1 recipe *Two-Egg Pasta* (page 12), rolled into 4 (6x12x$^1/_8$-inch) sheets

4 tablespoons butter, softened

$^1/_3$ cup hot cream

1 tablespoon white truffle oil

1 small white truffle, if desired

1 cup grated Parmigiano-Reggiano or dry Monterey Jack cheese (4 oz.)

Kosher (coarse) salt to taste

Freshly ground pepper to taste

2 cups *Chicken Stock* (page 22)

4 egg yolks

1 tablespoon minced snipped chives

❶ Heat oven to 375°F. Pierce potatoes with fork in several places; bake 50 to 60 minutes or until completely tender. Remove from oven and let cool until easy to handle; potatoes should still be hot. Reduce heat to 200°F. Using hands, break both potatoes in half crosswise. Set one half of potato in potato ricer, flesh side down. Press potato through ricer into dry ovenproof skillet; remove and discard skin. Repeat until all potatoes have been riced.

❷ Meanwhile, place celery root in medium saucepan over medium heat; add water 2 inches above celery root. Bring to a boil. Reduce heat to low and simmer about 25 minutes or until celery root is tender. Drain and rinse; drain again thoroughly. Pass celery root through ricer into dry sauté pan with potatoes. Bake vegetables 15 to 20 minutes or until very dry; stir occasionally. Do not let them brown. Place vegetables into medium bowl.

❸ Prepare Two-Egg Pasta. Cut pasta into 8 (6x6-inch) squares. Set squares on work surface and cover with clean kitchen towel.

❹ Mix 2 tablespoons of the butter, one-half of the cream and one-half of the truffle oil into vegetables. Mixture should be fairly dense (if it seems too thick, add remaining cream). If using truffle, mince one-third of it and fold into potato mixture; add cheese. Season with salt and pepper. Place potato mixture into pastry bag without tip.

❺ Pour Chicken Stock into wide saucepan or large skillet. Add 2 cups water and set pan over low heat. Fill small bowl with water and have small pastry brush at hand. Set 1 pasta square in center of work surface and pipe one-fourth of potato mixture in a 1-inch circle, leaving empty space about 1³/4 inches across in center. Carefully place 1 egg yolk into center; sprinkle ³/4 teaspoon chives on top. Brush edges with water. Set second pasta square on top; carefully fit around potato mixture and press to bottom square, gently pressing out any air and being careful not to break egg yolk. Be absolutely certain pasta squares are sealed together; use pastry cutter or paring knife to cut away edges, leaving a circle about 1 inch wide around filling. Fill remaining ravioli.

❻ In small saucepan, melt remaining 2 tablespoons butter over low heat. Warm 4 soup plates. Increase heat under chicken stock until simmering; cook each ravioli 2 minutes, spooning hot liquid over top if not fully submerged. Carefully transfer ravioli to soup plates. Pour 2 teaspoons butter over each one, drizzle with remaining truffle oil and sprinkle with remaining chives. If using truffle, use vegetable peeler to make very thin slices; scatter over ravioli.

4 servings.

Preparation time: 2 hours.

Ready to serve: 2 hours, 10 minutes.

Per serving: 625 calories, 37 g total fat (19 g saturated fat), 340 mg cholesterol, 1310 mg sodium, 4 g fiber.

Fresh fruit for dessert adds a light and lovely finishing touch.

CHEVRE LASAGNA

Lighter than traditional versions, this lasagna evokes flavors of the south of France: tangy goat cheese, pungent garlic, rich olives, fragrant olive oil.

	Tomato-Onion Sauce (recipe follows)
1	tablespoon kosher (coarse) salt
1	recipe *One-Egg Pasta* (page 11) in wide strips, or 8 dried large lasagna noodles
1 to 2	tablespoons olive oil
8	garlic cloves, thinly sliced
1/2	cup extra-virgin olive oil
3	cups young chèvre cheese (12 oz.)
1	cup oil-cured black olives, pitted, cut in half lengthwise
4	tablespoons minced fresh Italian parsley
1 1/2	cups fresh bread crumbs, toasted

❶ Prepare Tomato-Onion Sauce; set aside.

❷ Fill large pot two-thirds full of water; add 1 tablespoon salt. Bring to a boil over high heat. If using fresh pasta, cook 1 minute; carefully remove pasta and unfurl strips onto parchment paper brushed with olive oil. If using dried pasta, cook according to package directions. Drain; rinse in cool water. Drain again and set strips onto oiled parchment paper. Put garlic into small saucepan; cover with olive oil. Cook over very low heat 2 to 3 minutes or until garlic just begins to simmer.

❸ Heat oven to 350°F. To assemble lasagna, brush 3-quart dish with olive oil; cover bottom of dish with thin layer of sauce. Place noodles on sauce, setting them next to each other, but not overlapping. Crumble one-third of the chèvre over noodles; sprinkle one-third of the olives and parsley over cheese. Spoon one-third of the garlic and olive oil over olive layer. Spoon sauce on top; add another layer of noodles. Repeat until all ingredients have been used, ending with layer of noodles, sauce and bread crumbs.

❹ Cover dish tightly with aluminum foil; bake about 20 minutes or until cheese is hot and bubbly. Let stand 5 to 10 minutes before serving.

6 servings.
Preparation time: 1 hour. Ready to serve: 1 hour, 30 minutes.

Per serving: 1050 calories, 70 g total fat (24 g saturated fat), 155 mg cholesterol, 1550 mg sodium, 7 g fiber.

TOMATO-ONION SAUCE

    3   tablespoons olive oil
    2   yellow onions, cut into small dice
    6   garlic cloves, minced
        Kosher (coarse) salt to taste
        Freshly ground pepper to taste
    1   (28-oz.) can diced tomatoes

❶ In medium skillet, heat olive oil over medium-high heat; add onions. Sauté 15 to 20 minutes or until very soft and fragrant. Add garlic; sauté an additional 2 minutes. Season with salt and pepper. Stir in tomatoes; simmer 5 minutes. Remove from heat. Refrigerate until ready to use.

6 servings.
Preparation time: 5 minutes.
Ready to serve: 30 minutes.

Per serving: 105 calories, 7 g total fat (1 g saturated fat), 0 mg cholesterol, 220 mg sodium, 2 g fiber.

The delightfully tart flavor of Chèvre Lasagna *creates a lively contrast with a semisweet white wine, such as an Italian Lambrusco.*

OASTED CHICKEN WITH ORZO DRESSING

If you love orzo, you'll really enjoy this different take on poultry dressing.

1 tablespoon kosher (coarse) salt plus more to taste
6 oz. orzo or other small seed-shaped pasta
2 tablespoons olive oil
3 oz. pancetta, diced
1/2 cup Zante currants, soaked in hot water 15 minutes
1/8 teaspoon saffron
1/2 cup pine nuts, toasted
1 tablespoon grated lemon peel
2 tablespoons fresh lemon juice
3 tablespoons minced Italian parsley
  Freshly ground pepper to taste
1 (4 1/2- to 5-lb.) free-range chicken

❶ Fill large pot two-thirds full of water; add 1 tablespoon salt. Bring to a boil over high heat. Cook orzo according to package directions. Rinse and drain. In medium bowl, drizzle 1 tablespoon of the olive oil over cooked pasta; toss to coat evenly.

❷ Fry pancetta in small skillet over medium heat about 7 minutes or until translucent. Toss with pasta. Drain currants; add to pasta. In small bowl, add 2 teaspoons hot water to saffron; let stand 5 minutes. Add to pasta along with pine nuts, lemon peel, lemon juice and parsley; season with salt and pepper. Toss mixture.

❸ Heat oven to 325°F. Rinse chicken in cool water inside and out; drain thoroughly. Dry with clean kitchen towel. Season inside with salt and pepper. Fill both cavities of chicken with pasta stuffing; thread 2 water-soaked wooden skewers through flaps of chicken to close both openings. Brush skin of chicken with remaining 1 tablespoon olive oil. Set chicken on roasting rack over roasting pan; cover with tent of aluminum foil. Bake 1 1/4 to 1 1/2 hours or until internal temperature reaches 180°F.

④ Let chicken stand, covered with foil, 10 to 15 minutes before carving. Arrange carved meat on platter with stuffing in center.

6 servings.
Preparation time: 30 minutes. Ready to serve: 2 to 2^1/$_2$ hours.

Per serving: 730 calories, 45 g total fat (12 g saturated fat), 140 mg cholesterol, 590 mg sodium, 3 g fiber.

EASY CHEESE RAVIOLI WITH CARAMELIZED ONION AND WINTER SQUASH SAUCE

Using won ton wrappers cuts considerable time off the process of making raviolis, and results in a good, delicate pasta dish.

3	tablespoons *Clarified Butter* (page 18)
2	yellow onions, diced
1	tablespoon kosher (coarse) salt plus more to taste
	Freshly ground pepper to taste
1½	cups feta cheese, crumbled (6 oz.)
1½	cups fresh ricotta cheese (6 oz.)
1	cup freshly grated Parmigiano-Reggiano cheese (4 oz.)
1	egg yolk
1	tablespoon minced fresh Italian parsley
2	tablespoons minced fresh sage
30	won ton wrappers
4	oz. pancetta, diced
1	cup mashed baked winter squash
1½	cups *Chicken Stock* (page 22)
2	teaspoons olive oil
4 to 6	sage sprigs

❶ In medium skillet, melt Clarified Butter over medium-high heat; sauté onions 5 to 7 minutes or until wilted. Reduce heat to very low; season with salt and pepper. Sauté very slowly, stirring occasionally, about 1 hour or until onions are nearly melted and very sweet.

❷ Meanwhile, combine cheeses in medium bowl. Add egg yolk, parsley and 1 tablespoon of the sage; mix thoroughly.

❸ To make ravioli, set 4 won ton wrappers on work surface. Add about 1 tablespoon filling in center of each wrapper. Using index finger, brush edges with a little water. Top with second won ton wrapper; press edges together with fork. Repeat until all filling is used. Set filled ravioli on

parchment paper-lined 13x9-inch pan; cover with plastic wrap and clean kitchen towel. Refrigerate until ready to cook.

❹ Fry pancetta in large skillet over medium-high heat until completely translucent. Stir in caramelized onions, winter squash purée and Chicken Stock. Add remaining 1 tablespoon sage; season with salt and pepper. Simmer 10 minutes; remove from heat.

❺ Fill large pot two-thirds full of water; add 1 tablespoon salt and olive oil. Bring to a boil over high heat. Cook ravioli about 4 minutes per batch, removing from boiling water when they begin to turn translucent. Keep cooked ravioli warm as you cook remainder.

❻ Divide ravioli evenly among plates; spoon sauce over each portion. Garnish with sage sprigs.

4 servings.
Preparation time: 1 hour, 15 minutes. Ready to serve: 1 hour, 30 minutes.
Per serving: 850 calories, 60 g total fat (30 g saturated fat), 210 mg cholesterol, 1535 mg sodium, 4 g fiber.

PUMPKIN AND ROASTED GARLIC CANNELLONI WITH CHÈVRE SAUCE

3	cups *Chèvre Sauce* (recipe follows on page 140)
2	garlic bulbs, paper skins removed, washed thoroughly
1/2	cup plus 2 tablespoons olive oil
9	rosemary sprigs
9	sage sprigs
1	(3-lb.) winter squash, such as Kabosha, Delicata, Tahitian Melon, Lakota or Sugar Pumpkin (do not use carving pumpkin)
1	tablespoon minced fresh sage
1/2	teaspoon minced fresh rosemary
1	teaspoon freshly ground nutmeg
	Kosher (coarse) salt to taste
	Freshly ground pepper to taste
1/2	teaspoon chipotle powder, if desired
18	(5x5-inch) squares pumpkin or squid-ink pasta, or both, to make cannelloni

❶ Prepare Chèvre Sauce; set aside.

❷ Heat oven to 325°F. Bake garlic and squash at same time. To prepare garlic, in small deep ovenproof covered dish, pour 1/2 cup of the olive oil over garlic, one of the rosemary sprigs and one of the sage sprigs. Add enough water to come halfway up garlic bulbs. Season with salt and pepper. Cover and bake about 45 minutes or until garlic is completely soft and tender. Let garlic cool slightly; remove from cooking liquid. Cool to room temperature.

❸ To prepare winter squash, cut squash in half lengthwise using large heavy-duty knife. Use spoon to scrape out seeds and fibers. Brush cut surfaces with remaining 2 tablespoons olive oil; place on baking sheet. Bake 45 to 90 minutes or until tender when pierced with fork. Cool to room temperature.

❹ Scoop flesh from squash; put in medium bowl. Mash well with fork. Using thumb, pull root from each garlic bulb. Set garlic on clean work surface; press down on it slowly with heel of hand so that soft pulp comes out of

each clove. Use fork to mash garlic into fine purée; add to squash. Mix thoroughly. Add minced sage, minced rosemary and nutmeg; season with salt and pepper. Stir in chipotle powder. (Filling can be prepared up to 2 days in advance.) Cover and refrigerate.

5 To assemble cannelloni, set several squares of pasta on work surface. Spread about 4 tablespoons pumpkin mixture over each square, leaving 1/4-inch margin on all sides. Roll up loosely; repeat until all squares are filled.

6 Heat oven to 350°F. Spread 1/2 cup sauce into 3-quart casserole. Place cannelloni in sauce, seam side down; pour remaining sauce evenly over cannelloni, reserving 3/4 cup. Cover dish tightly with aluminum foil; bake 15 to 20 minutes or until cannelloni are heated through and pasta is tender.

7 Heat reserved sauce; place 3 cannelloni on each plate and spoon reserved sauce over each portion. Garnish with sprigs of rosemary and sage; grind pepper over each portion.

6 servings.

Preparation time: 1 hour, 30 minutes. Ready to serve: 2 hours, 15 minutes.

Per serving: 875 calories, 49 g total fat (30 g saturated fat), 245 mg cholesterol, 855 mg sodium, 9 g fiber.

Continued on page 140

Continued from page 139

CHEVRE SAUCE

   3   cups whipping cream
   2   cups fresh chèvre cheese (8 oz.)
   3   tablespoons minced Italian parsley
       Kosher (coarse) salt to taste
       Freshly ground pepper to taste

1 Heat cream to a boil in 3-quart saucepan over medium heat. Reduce heat to medium-low; simmer about 10 minutes or until cream is reduced by one-third. Stir in chèvre and parsley; season with salt and pepper. When sauce is heated through, remove from heat. Refrigerate sauce if it will stand more than 30 minutes.

6 servings.

Preparation time: 15 minutes. Ready to serve: 15 minutes.

Per serving (¼ cup): 450 calories, 45 g total fat (29 g saturated fat), 166 mg cholesterol, 170 mg sodium, .06 g fiber.

TIPS FOR MAKING CANNELLONI

Begin with fresh pasta sheets about $1/16$-inch thick and 5 inches square; do not cook them first.

Allow 2 to 3 cannelloni per serving.

Prepare filling the morning or even the day before making cannelloni.

Allow 4 tablespoons of filling per cannelloni.

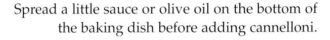

Spread a little sauce or olive oil on the bottom of the baking dish before adding cannelloni.

Be certain that the pasta itself is completely covered with sauce.

Cover dish tightly with aluminum foil; this will ensure that the pasta is fully cooked and tender.

Bake no more than 15 to 20 minutes. If a filling requires a longer cooking time, cook the filling partially before you fill cannelloni.

141

MACARONI AND CHEESE WITH TOMATOES AND FONTINA

I don't know anyone who can resist good macaroni and cheese. Here, tomatoes contribute a lively, acidic element. Vegetarians can omit the pancetta, or replace it with minced and sautéed portobello mushrooms.

1   tablespoon kosher (coarse) salt plus more to taste
1   lb. canneroni, trennete or other medium tube pasta
6   oz. pancetta, minced
1   (12-oz.) can evaporated milk
1/2   cup whipping cream
1   (14-oz.) can diced tomatoes
1   tablespoon hot pepper sauce
    Freshly ground pepper to taste
5   cups shredded or grated Monterey Jack cheese (20 oz.)
3   cups shredded or grated Italian fontina cheese (12 oz.)
2   cups fresh bread crumbs, toasted

❶ Fill large pot two-thirds full of water; add 1 tablespoon salt. Bring to a boil over high heat. Cook canneroni according to package directions; drain. Do not rinse.

❷ Meanwhile, in medium skillet over medium heat, sauté pancetta until translucent, about 5 minutes. Remove from heat; set aside.

❸ Heat oven to 350°F. In large bowl, combine evaporated milk, cream, tomatoes and hot pepper sauce. Season with pepper. Fold in cheeses. Add pasta and pancetta to cheese mixture; stir together gently but thoroughly.

❹ Pour pasta mixture into 3 1/2-quart casserole. Season bread crumbs with salt and pepper; spread over pasta. Cover tightly with aluminum foil; bake 20 minutes. Remove foil; bake an additional 10 minutes or until bread crumbs are lightly toasted. Remove from oven; let stand 5 minutes before serving.

8 servings.

Preparation time: 15 minutes. Ready to serve: 45 minutes.

Per serving: 1275 calories, 85 g total fat (45 g saturated fat), 210 mg cholesterol, 1660 mg sodium, 4 g fiber.

PASTA FRITTATA

A frittata with pasta is a close cousin of the Spanish tapa, Tortilla Española, a thick, unfolded potato omelette served cut into wedges. I've made this with pasta noodles such as angel hair, but it is easier to cut and serve when made with seed-shaped pasta. It is delicious hot from the stove, but it is also excellent the next day, chilled, and is perfect in a lunch box.

1 tablespoon kosher (coarse) salt plus more to taste

8 oz. orzo (seed-shaped pasta)

3 tablespoons olive oil

1 yellow onion, diced

4 oz. pancetta, minced

   Freshly ground pepper to taste

1/2 teaspoon crushed red pepper

8 eggs

1/4 cup minced fresh herbs such as oregano, thyme, marjoram
   or Italian parsley

1 cup freshly grated dry Monterey Jack or Parmigiano-Reggiano
   cheese (4 oz.)

❶ Fill large pot two-thirds full of water; add 1 tablespoon salt. Bring to a boil over high heat. Cook orzo according to package directions; drain. Rinse and drain pasta thoroughly in cool water. Drizzle with 1 tablespoon of the olive oil; toss gently. Set pasta aside.

❷ Meanwhile, in medium skillet, heat another 1 tablespoon olive oil over medium-high heat until hot; sauté onion 5 minutes or until very soft and fragrant. Add pancetta; cook an additional 5 minutes or until pancetta is translucent. Season with pepper and 1/2 teaspoon crushed red pepper; remove from heat. Cool slightly.

❸ Heat oven to 375°F. In large bowl, stir together eggs, pasta, herbs, cheese, and onion mixture; season with salt and pepper. Rinse skillet and wipe dry. Coat sides and bottom of pan with remaining 1 tablespoon olive oil. Set pan over medium-high heat. Pour egg mixture into pan. Cook 5 to 15

minutes or until frittata forms light golden-brown crust at edge and is nearly set inside. Use rubber spatula to loosen sides and bottom occasionally.

❹ Transfer frittata to oven. Bake 12 minutes or until cooked through. Remove from oven; carefully loosen frittata using a rubber spatula. Transfer to serving plate. Let stand 2 minutes; cut into wedges. Or cool frittata to room temperature before serving.

6 to 8 servings.

Preparation time: 20 minutes. Ready to serve: 45 minutes.

Per serving: 570 calories, 38 g total fat (13 g saturated fat), 315 mg cholesterol, 670 mg sodium, 1.75 g fiber.

TURKEY RAVIOLI WITH SAGE CREAM SAUCE

You must make raviolis using fresh pasta; there is no dried substitute. You can make your own, of course. Or if there is a store near you that sells fresh pasta, ask if they will reserve whole sheets for you. Most stores cut their pasta in advance, but if you ask they are usually willing to save you some for raviolis, cannelloni or lasagna.

2   tablespoons butter

3   shallots, minced

1   garlic clove, minced

2   tablespoons minced fresh sage

3/4   lb. cooked dark turkey meat, minced, or 1 lb. ground turkey

1   tablespoon kosher (coarse) salt plus more to taste
    Freshly ground pepper to taste

1   egg white

1   recipe *One-Egg Pasta* (page 11), rolled into sheets about
        1/8-inch thick

3   cups half-and-half

3   fresh sage sprigs

❶ Melt butter in medium skillet over medium heat until foamy; add shallots. Sauté 5 to 6 minutes or until soft and transparent. Add garlic and minced sage; sauté an additional 1 minute. Set aside one-third of mixture.

❷ Stir minced turkey into remaining two-thirds of shallot mixture. (If using ground turkey, add it to remaining two-thirds of shallot mixture; sauté over medium-high heat until ground turkey is no longer pink in center. Drain and discard fat.) Cool turkey mixture to room temperature. Season with salt and pepper.

❸ In small bowl, whisk egg white with 1 tablespoon water. To make ravioli, set 1 sheet pasta on work surface. Use ruler to score and cut pasta into 24 squares, each just slightly larger than 2 1/2 x 2 1/2 inches. Fill 12 squares each with 1 teaspoon filling; brush edges with egg wash. Top with remaining 12 squares pasta. Use tines of fork to seal edges of ravioli. Set

filled raviolis on parchment paper; cover with clean kitchen towel. Repeat until all raviolis are prepared.

4 Heat reserved one-third shallot mixture in $2^1/_2$-quart saucepan. Add half-and-half and 1 sage sprig; bring to a boil over medium heat. Reduce heat to low; simmer about 15 minutes or until half-and-half is reduced by one-third. Remove and discard sage sprig; season mixture with salt and pepper. Set aside.

5 Fill large pot two-thirds full of water; add 1 tablespoon salt. Heat to boiling over high heat. Cook raviolis in batches about 4 minutes or until pasta is tender. You will need to work quickly so raviolis do not stick to each other. Drain cooked raviolis; divide evenly among plates. Spoon sage cream sauce over each portion; garnish with remaining fresh sage sprigs. Grind pepper over each portion.

16 servings.
Preparation time: 1 hour. Ready to serve: 1 hour, 10 minutes.

Per serving: 635 calories, 40 g total fat (20 g saturated fat), 210 mg cholesterol, 600 mg sodium, 1 g fiber.

SWISS CHARD CANNELLONI WITH SPICY TOMATO SAUCE

Swiss chard has a richness and intensity that goes beautifully with the spicy complexity of this tomato sauce. For a perfect accompaniment, try a Zinfandel — a red one! — from Dry Creek Valley in Sonoma County.

4	cups Spicy Tomato Sauce (recipe follows)
4	cups sliced Swiss chard
2	tablespoons olive oil
1/2	cup chopped onion
4	garlic cloves, minced
1/4	teaspoon crushed red pepper
	Freshly ground pepper to taste
3	cups fresh ricotta (12 oz.)
1/4	lb. prosciutto, minced
1	cup grated dry Monterey Jack cheese (4 oz.)
2	eggs, beaten
18	(5x5-inch) squares spinach pasta

❶ Prepare Spicy Tomato Sauce; set aside.

❷ Stack chard leaves on work surface; cut into 1/4-inch crosswise strips. Heat olive oil in large skillet over medium-high heat; add onion. Sauté about 10 minutes or until soft and fragrant. Add garlic and crushed red pepper; sauté an additional 2 minutes. Add chard; cover pan. Cook 5 minutes or until wilted; season with salt and pepper. Remove from heat.

❸ In medium bowl, combine ricotta, prosciutto, Monterey Jack cheese and eggs; mix thoroughly. Fold in chard mixture.

❹ To assemble cannelloni, set several squares of pasta on work surface. Spread about 4 tablespoons chard mixture over each square, leaving 1/4-inch margin on all sides. Roll up loosely; repeat until all squares are filled, about 3 cups.

❺ Heat oven to 350°F. Spread 1/2 cup sauce into 3-quart casserole. Place cannelloni in sauce, seam side down; pour remaining sauce evenly over

cannelloni, reserving ³/₄ cup. Cover tightly with aluminum foil; bake
15 minutes or until cannelloni are heated through and pasta is tender.

⑥ Heat reserved sauce; place 3 cannelloni on each plate. Spoon reserved sauce
over each portion.

6 servings.

Preparation time: 20 minutes. Ready to serve: 1 hour.

Per serving: 585 calories, 25 g total fat (9 g saturated fat), 165 mg cholesterol, 2200 mg sodium, 6 g fiber.

SPICY TOMATO SAUCE

2	tablespoons olive oil
1	yellow onion, minced
2	garlic cloves, minced
	Kosher (coarse) salt to taste
	Freshly ground pepper to taste
1	teaspoon fresh ground nutmeg
¹/₈	teaspoon ground cloves
¹/₂	teaspoon ground cinnamon
¹/₂	teaspoon crushed red pepper
¹/₂	cup white wine
2	(14-oz.) cans tomato sauce

❶ Heat olive oil in medium skillet over medium-high heat until hot; sauté
onion about 5 minutes or until soft and fragrant. Add garlic; sauté an
additional 2 minutes. Season with salt, pepper and 1 teaspoon nutmeg;
stir in cloves, cinnamon and crushed red pepper.

❷ Add wine; reduce heat to low. Simmer about 4 minutes or until wine is
reduced by one-half. Stir in tomato sauce; reduce heat. Simmer 20 minutes.
Season with salt and pepper, if desired.

2¹/₂ cups.

Preparation time: 5 minutes. Ready to serve: 45 minutes.

Per cup: 70 calories, 4 g total fat (.5 g saturated fat), 0 mg cholesterol, 895 mg sodium, 2 g fiber.

SMOKED SUMMER VEGETABLES WITH SAUSAGES AND CAVATAPPI

It is easiest to smoke vegetables the morning or even the day before making the sauce. And you can make the entire sauce beforehand, if you like. It will give the flavors a chance to meld. Any commercial home smoker should give detailed instructions for smoking meats, poultry and vegetables.

    1 large eggplant, cut in half lengthwise
    2 yellow onions, cut in half crosswise
    6 plum tomatoes
    1 tablespoon kosher (coarse) salt plus more to taste
    1 lb. cavatappi pasta
    1 lb. Italian sausage, casings removed
    3 tablespoons olive oil
    6 garlic cloves, minced
    1 cup dry white wine
  1/4 cup minced fresh Italian parsley
1/2 to 1 teaspoon crushed red pepper
       Freshly ground pepper to taste
  11/2 cups shredded smoked mozzarella (6 oz.)
  11/2 cups fresh bread crumbs, toasted

❶ Prepare smoker according to manufacturer's instructions and smoke vegetables. Or, roast vegetables in 15x10-inch baking pan at 400°F oven for 30 minutes. When smoked, peel eggplant and cut into 3/4-inch dice. Dice onions and toss with eggplant in medium bowl. Peel tomatoes, cut in half, remove seeds and gel; mince. Put in small bowl. Cover vegetables and refrigerate until ready to make sauce.

❷ Fill large pot two-thirds full of water; add 1 tablespoon salt. Bring to a boil over high heat. Cook cavatappi according to package directions; drain. Do not rinse. Transfer cooked pasta to large bowl. Heat oven to 375°F.

❸ Meanwhile, cook sausage in large skillet over medium heat, using fork to crumble, about 7 to 8 minutes or until sausage is no longer pink in center.

Pour off fat; transfer sausage to small bowl. Return pan to medium-low heat; add olive oil, eggplant and onions. Sauté, stirring frequently, 15 to 20 minutes or until very tender. Do not let vegetables brown. Add garlic, sauté an additional 2 minutes. Add tomatoes; simmer 2 minutes. Add wine; simmer 5 to 6 minutes or until reduced by two-thirds. Stir in cooked sausage, parsley and crushed red pepper; season with salt and pepper.

4 Toss sauce with pasta; add cheese and toss quickly. Pour mixture into 3-quart casserole; spread bread crumbs over top. Bake about 20 minutes or until mixture is hot and bubbly and top is just turning golden brown. Let stand 5 to 10 minutes before serving.

6 servings.
Preparation time: 25 minutes. Ready to serve: 45 minutes, plus smoking time.
Per serving: 660 calories, 26 g total fat (9 g saturated fat), 55 mg cholesterol, 1120 mg sodium, 7 g fiber.

$\int$USILLI COL BUCO WITH LAMB RAGU

This voluptuous sauce requires long cooking, though you needn't do anything but stir it occasionally to ensure it doesn't burn. It is traditionally served with papardelle, and to do so you'll need two (8.8 oz.) packages. In this version, I've used long "springs" because twists in pasta hold little morsels of meat and vegetables beautifully.

3	tablespoons extra-virgin olive oil
1	yellow onion, minced
3	carrots, peeled, minced
3	ribs celery, minced
6	oz. pancetta, diced
2	lbs. ground lamb
1	tablespoon kosher (coarse) salt plus more to taste
	Freshly ground pepper to taste
1	teaspoon cinnamon
1	teaspoon freshly ground nutmeg
1½	cups dry white wine
1	cup whole milk
3	cups canned diced tomatoes
½	cup whipping cream
1	(17.6-oz.) pkg. fusilli col buco or fusilli lunghi (spring-shaped pasta)
½	cup freshly grated Parmigiano-Reggiano cheese (2 oz.)

❶ Heat olive oil in large skillet over medium-low heat until hot. Add onion; sauté about 10 minutes or until soft. Add carrots and celery; sauté 20 to 25 minutes or until vegetables are very soft. Add pancetta; sauté 7 to 8 minutes or until translucent; discard fat. Add lamb; increase heat to medium. Sauté, stirring constantly with fork, until lamb is no longer pink in center. Season with salt and pepper; add cinnamon and nutmeg.

❷ Stir in wine; simmer about 15 minutes or until nearly evaporated. Add milk; simmer about 10 minutes or until nearly evaporated. Stir in tomatoes;

reduce heat to very low. Cook slowly 4 to 5 hours, stirring occasionally. After sauce has been cooking 3 hours, use large spoon to skim off and discard fat. Continue to cook until sauce is very thick and rich. Thirty minutes before serving, stir in cream.

❸ Fill large pot two-thirds full of water; add 1 tablespoon salt. Bring to a boil over high heat. Cook fusilli col buco according to package directions; drain. Do not rinse. Transfer cooked pasta to large bowl. Add 2 cups sauce; toss. Divide pasta evenly among bowls or plates. Top each serving with a generous spoonful of sauce and grated cheese.

6 servings.

Preparation time: 30 minutes. Ready to serve: 4 hours.

Per serving: 875 calories, 40 g total fat (16.5 g saturated fat), 130 mg cholesterol, 1110 mg sodium, 6 g fiber.

FAZZOLETTI WITH CHEVRE AND SHREDDED RADICCHIO

Fazzoletti are handkerchiefs of fresh pasta. They are pretty, with tender folds, and not at all difficult to make once you master getting the pasta out of the water without it tearing. A broad, flat, slotted spoon works best.

1 recipe *Two-Egg Pasta* (page 12)
2 tablespoons olive oil
1 shallot, minced
3 oz. pancetta, diced
1 (10- to 12-oz.) head radicchio, cored, shredded
1/3 cup balsamic vinegar
1 tablespoon kosher (coarse) salt plus more to taste
    Freshly ground pepper to taste
2 cups young chèvre cheese such as fromage blanc or chabis (8 oz.)
2 tablespoons fresh-snipped chives
1/3 cup extra-virgin olive oil

❶ Prepare Two-Egg Pasta. Cut into 24 (4-inch) squares and set aside to dry, covered with a clean kitchen towel, about 15 minutes.

❷ Heat 2 tablespoons olive oil in large skillet over medium-low heat; add shallot. Sauté 5 to 6 minutes or until soft. Add pancetta; sauté 5 to 6 minutes or until translucent. Add radicchio; toss. Add balsamic vinegar. Cover pan 3 to 4 minutes or until radicchio is wilted. Uncover; stir and season with salt and pepper. Remove from heat and set aside.

❸ Fill large pot two-thirds full of water; add 1 tablespoon salt. Bring to a boil over high heat. When water boils, cook pasta in batches until it is just tender, about 2 minutes. When one batch is cooked, quickly set each square on clean work surface. Place 1 tablespoon (about 3/8 oz.) chèvre in center, sprinkle with chives, fold in half diagonally, and bring bottom corners together to form small triangle. Set 4 to 6 filled fazzoletti on individual warmed plates and keep warm while making next batch. Continue until all of fazzoletti have been made.

④ Working quickly, return radicchio mixture to medium heat. Stir in extra-virgin olive oil; heat through. Season to taste; spoon sauce over each portion.

4 to 6 servings.
Preparation time: 45 minutes. Ready to serve: 1 hour, 10 minutes.

Per serving: 850 calories, 60 g total fat (20 g saturated fat), 175 mg cholesterol, 920 mg sodium, 3 g fiber.

ROASTED GARLIC AND PASTA SOUFFLE

Pasta contributes structure and volume to a delicate soufflé, an element that is helpful to beginners who are distressed when efforts collapse, as all soufflés do (they're supposed to!). If you've been reluctant to try your hand at making a soufflé, you'll enjoy the perky resilience of this one, which does not fall as much as most others.

2 garlic bulbs, cleaned
1/4 cup olive oil
2 thyme sprigs
1 tablespoon kosher (coarse) salt plus more to taste
Freshly ground pepper to taste
6 oz. acini di pepe (peppercorn-shaped pasta)
2 teaspoons butter, softened
2 oz. pancetta, diced
2 cups whipping cream
6 eggs, separated
2 teaspoons crushed red pepper
3 tablespoons minced Italian parsley
1 cup grated or shredded Italian fontina cheese (4 oz.)
1/2 cup grated pecorino cheese (2 oz.)

❶ Heat oven to 375°F. Remove outer skins from garlic, leaving bulbs intact. In small baking dish, pour olive oil over garlic bulbs and thyme. Season with salt and pepper; add 1/4 cup water. Cover dish tightly with aluminum foil; bake about 1 hour or until garlic is tender. Remove bulbs from cooking liquid; cool to room temperature. Reserve cooking liquid.

❷ Fill large pot two-thirds full of water; add 1 tablespoon salt. Bring to a boil over high heat. Cook acini di pepe according to package directions; drain. Rinse and drain pasta thoroughly in cool water. In medium bowl, drizzle 1 tablespoon garlic cooking liquid over pasta; toss until evenly coated.

❸ Butter 2 1/2-quart soufflé dish. In medium saucepan, cook pancetta over medium-high heat 4 to 5 minutes or until almost crisp; drain fat. Add

cream; simmer until reduced by one-third, about 5 minutes. Cool to room temperature, about 30 minutes.

❹ In medium bowl, beat egg yolks with whisk until pale yellow and thick. Add 1 teaspoon of the crushed red pepper and parsley; season with salt and pepper. Pour in cream mixture; fold in cheeses.

❺ In large bowl, whisk egg whites until soft peaks form. Using rubber spatula, fold one-third of the egg whites into egg yolk mixture; fold in pasta and remaining egg whites. Do not overmix. Pour mixture into soufflé dish; dust surface with remaining 1 teaspoon crushed red pepper.

❻ Bake soufflé 25 minutes; reduce oven temperature to 325°F. Bake an additional 40 minutes or until puffy and set and top is just turning golden brown. Remove from oven and serve immediately.

6 servings.

Preparation time: 1 hour, 30 minutes. Ready to serve: 2 hours, 45 minutes.

Per serving: 1005 calories, 78 g total fat (42 g saturated fat), 520 mg cholesterol, 1180 mg sodium, 2 g fiber.

SWEET POTATO RAVIOLI WITH WALNUT SAUCE

Sometimes familiar foods served in a new context enliven a traditional meal and lend a festive air. Serving ravioli as a first course on Thanksgiving is a perfect example. You can prepare this recipe the day before serving; just be sure to cover tightly with plastic wrap so pasta does not become dry.

FILLING

- 1 sweet potato (14 oz.)
- 1 Russet potato (6 oz.)
- 2 tablespoons butter, softened
  Kosher (coarse) salt to taste
  Freshly ground pepper to taste
- 3/4 cup freshly grated Parmigiano-Reggiano cheese (3 oz.)
- 3 tablespoons minced fresh Italian parsley
- 1/2 cup walnuts, toasted, minced

SAUCE

- 3 tablespoons butter
- 1 small shallot, minced
- 3 garlic cloves, minced
- 3 tablespoons toasted chopped walnuts
- 1 cup whipping cream
- 3/4 cup freshly grated Parmigiano-Reggiano cheese (3 oz.)
- 2 tablespoons minced fresh Italian parsley
- 1 tablespoon kosher (coarse) salt plus more to taste
  Freshly ground pepper to taste

RAVIOLI

- 1 egg white
- 2 pkg. won ton wrappers

❶ Heat oven to 375°F. Pierce potatoes with fork in several places. Bake 50 to 60 minutes or until completely tender. Remove potatoes from oven; cool until easy to handle, but still hot. Using hands, break both potatoes in half crosswise. Set one half in ricer, flesh side down. Press potato through ricer into medium bowl; remove and discard skin. Repeat until both potatoes have been riced. Add butter to potatoes; mix until well incorporated. Season with salt and pepper; fold in cheese, parsley and walnuts.

❷ To prepare sauce, in medium saucepan melt butter over medium-high heat. Add shallot; sauté 3 minutes. Add garlic and sauté an additional 2 minutes. Stir in walnuts and sauté 1 minute. Pour in cream; heat through. Reduce heat to low; simmer 4 minutes. Stir in cheese and parsley; season with salt and pepper. Set sauce aside.

❸ In small bowl, mix egg white with 1 tablespoon water. To make ravioli, fill 12 won ton wrappers each with 1 teaspoon filling; brush edges with egg wash and top with remaining 12 squares. Use tines of fork to press edges of each ravioli together to seal. Set filled raviolis on clean kitchen towel or parchment paper and cover. Repeat until all raviolis have been made.

❹ Fill large pot two-thirds full of water; add 1 tablespoon salt. Bring to a boil over high heat. Cook ravioli 2 minutes for homemade pasta, 3 to 4 minutes for commercial fresh pasta, 45 to 60 seconds for won ton wrappers or until pasta is just tender. Use slotted spoon to remove ravioli from water. Drain ravioli; divide evenly among plates; spoon sauce over each portion.

12 servings.
Preparation time: 1 hour, 30 minutes. Ready to serve: 1 hour, 45 minutes.

Per serving: 895 calories, 60 g total fat (30 g saturated fat), 170 mg cholesterol, 1260 mg sodium, 5 g fiber.

SPAGHETTI CARBONARA

For this classic version to work, the pasta must be very hot when it is added to the egg mixture, and you must begin to toss it immediately so that the eggs do not set.

1	tablespoon kosher (coarse) salt plus more to taste
12	oz. dried spaghetti or bucatini
3	oz. pancetta, diced
2	garlic cloves, minced
2	pasteurized eggs
2	pasteurized egg yolks
2	tablespoons minced fresh Italian parsley
3/4	cup grated Parmigiano-Reggiano cheese (3 oz.)
1/2	cup grated aged Italian Asiago or pecorino cheese (2 oz.)
	Freshly ground pepper to taste

❶ Fill large pot two-thirds full of water; add 1 tablespoon salt. Bring to a boil over high heat. Cook spaghetti according to package directions; drain. Do not rinse.

❷ Meanwhile, sauté pancetta in small skillet 3 minutes or until translucent and almost crisp; drain fat. Add garlic; sauté an additional 1 minute. Remove from heat.

❸ Beat eggs and yolks with wire whisk in deep bowl until eggs are smooth and slightly thickened. Add parsley, cheeses and pepper. Add pancetta and garlic; stir mixture with wooden spoon. Immediately add hot pasta to bowl and toss mixture, using two large pasta forks, until pasta is thoroughly coated with egg mixture. Season with salt and pepper. Divide pasta evenly among plates.

4 servings.
Preparation time: 10 minutes. Ready to serve: 20 minutes.
Per serving: 740 calories, 36 g total fat (16 g saturated fat), 260 mg cholesterol, 1420 mg sodium, 3 g fiber.

LASAGNA WITH LAMB RAGU

The actual hands-on work involved in this dish is moderate, but ragu must cook for a long time. Your efforts will be rewarded: the leftovers, warmed in the oven, are great.

　　Lamb Ragu (page 152)
　　Bechamel Sauce (page 18)
1　tablespoon kosher (coarse) salt
1　lb. dried lasagna noodles
1　tablespoon butter or olive oil
6　cups fresh ricotta (24 oz.)
4　cups fresh mozzarella, sliced (16 oz.)
1　cup grated Parmigiano-Reggiano cheese (4 oz.)

❶ Fill large pot two-thirds full of water; add 1 tablespoon salt. Bring to a boil over high heat. Cook lasagne according to package directions; drain. Rinse and drain pasta thoroughly. Spread noodles on one sheet parchment paper in a single layer.

❷ Heat oven to 375°F. Butter or oil 3-quart casserole; spread thin layer of prepared Bechamel Sauce over bottom of dish. Fold remainder of Bechamel into prepared Ragu.

❸ Layer lasagna noodles over Bechamel, arranging noodles tightly without overlapping. Sprinkle one-third of the ricotta over noodles; ladle one-third of the sauce over cheese. Add layer of noodles; top with one-third of the mozzarella and another one-third of the sauce. Continue until all noodles have been used. Top final layer of noodles with remaining sauce; sprinkle grated cheese on top.

❹ Cover dish with aluminum foil, sealing tightly around edges. Bake 20 minutes; remove foil and bake an additional 10 minutes. Remove from oven; let stand 10 minutes before serving.

12 to 15 servings.
Preparation time: 4 hours, 30 minutes. Ready to serve time: 1 hour.

Per serving: 1375 calories, 80 g total fat (41.5 g saturated fat), 270 mg cholesterol, 1815 mg sodium, 6 g fiber.

RECIPE INDEX

This index lists every recipe in Lotsa Pasta *by name. If you're looking for a specific recipe but can't recall the exact name, turn to the General Index that starts on page 164.*

GENERAL INDEX

There are several ways to use this helpful index. First — you can find recipes by name. If you don't know a recipe's specific name but recall a main ingredient or the cooking technique, look under that heading and all the related recipes will be listed; scan for the recipe you want. If you have an ingredient or cooking technique in mind and want to find a great recipe for it, look under that ingredient heading as well to find a list of recipes to choose from. Finally — you can use this general index to find a summary of the recipes in each chapter of the book (appetizers, soups, salads, etc.).